STEP UP TO SUCCESS

How to Grow A Novice Into

A Top Performer

By Jerry Isenhour

How to use this book:

Following each chapter, you will find a brief summary covering the main points of the chapter. After that, space is provided for you to write out questions that have been generated by the reading, and room for your answers as well as for notes. This is a workbook - you want to be engaged in what you are reading, making plans for how you will implement this in your business.

TABLE OF CONTENTS

Preface 1

Introduction And Foreword 3

The Blue-Collar-Worker/Skilled Trades Worker 13

Understanding The Generation Gap 19

Understand The Various Learning Styles 29

Additional Personality Types Commonly Found In
The Workplace 35

Recruiting People Who Can Be Effective Team Members 45

Training 55

Standard Operating Procedures 65

Onboarding (Day One) The Most Important Day Of
Their Career 71

The Training Process 77

Initial Basic Training 85

Outside/Off-Site Training 97

Contract Trainers 107

The Continuous Training Process 113

Ride-Along Training Process 121

The Validation Process 129

Certification And Licensing 137

Summary 147

About The Author 149

PREFACE

You've probably heard the old saying, "Those who can't do...teach."

While that phrase is an oft-repeated cliché, my personal experience is exactly the opposite. The best instructors are the ones who have the deepest knowledge base. High-performance teachers also provide something more: an extraordinary degree of insight into how to *apply* what they are imparting in the real world.

What you are about to read is a book jam-packed with knowledge about how to lead novices to attain success in the trades. But it's more than that. You're about to receive extraordinary insight into leadership, communication, and practical application about training, skill building, and so much more.

Part of what I love about this book is that it is a comprehensive manual for any blue-collar entrepreneur or manager. It will show you how to go from interviewing and on-boarding a brand-new employee all the way to guiding them through certification and licensing so they become "rock-star" team members. This is likely the only leadership guide any manager or leader in your industry will ever need.

However, there is a primary reason that I'm such a fan of this book – it's the author. My belief is that the best teachers are also extraordinary learners. Jerry Isenhour is the most serious student I have ever encountered…and there's probably no higher compliment that I could pay any professional.

Jerry is deeply committed to learning, which is part of what makes him such a profound teacher and author. He is that high-performing teacher and mentor who embodies the concept that those who are the best at their craft are the ones from whom we should be excited to learn.

Finally, you now have a comprehensive guide on how to take a prospective employee up to a rockstar for your business that is written by the best in the business.

It's time for YOU to "step up to success" so you can show your team members the way. Read this book…learn from it…and reap the benefits!

Scott McKain
Founder, The Distinction Institute
Professional Speakers Hall of Fame; Sales & Marketing Hall of Fame
Author of "ICONIC," "Create Distinction," and "What Customers REALLY Want."

INTRODUCTION AND FOREWORD

The original draft of this book was released in 2018. At the time, research on the available workforce was done. It was found that the overriding issue that businesses faced in the blue-collar trades was lower and lower availability of workers to join our teams. The people on our teams are the number 1 resource that any business owner has at their disposal, but finding those people was one of the leading frustrations that business owners often faced. This was common and due to many factors. People like Mike Rowe continued to preach that this dwindling workforce has been caused by our society's view that "dirty jobs", as many times skilled trades are now called, are looked down on. Every parent and secondary school seem to be driving our children to attain a college degree, a degree that, as many know, often results in long-term debt and attainment of skills that are not in demand and cannot be sold, or that there are more applicants than there are jobs.

This problem has only increased as of the second writing of this book in the latter part of 2020. In the year 2020, we faced a major pandemic that has left us with high unemployment, while at the same time the issue of finding, onboarding, and training of new hires exists, and many feel that it has escalated even beyond what we are witnessing in 2020. The demand from companies employing the blue-collar workforce has increased steadily, even as we pass through the pandemic into the post-pandemic world that we now view as the new normal. The procurement of work force members becomes a more difficult task each day, and only promises to continue to escalate and cause business stagnation. Due to this lack of a ready labor force, businesses cannot grow to the level desired by many owners and managers. Often, as we survey business owners, we find this is the number 1 challenge faced today, as it has been for several years. This likely can also be traced to record high unemployment compensation benefits that have left more and more employers competing against unemployment compensation, which has now become an adversary to building our teams.

We now see many individuals with college degrees that do not even work in the fields in which they invested their time, their training, and even years of their lives. Mike Rowe of "Dirty Jobs" fame has said this so many times: we are sending people to schools to obtain degrees for jobs they will never find and to obtain skills they cannot sell. This is due to many factors in the world today, but the plain truth is that technicians in many segments of the blue-collar world are sorely needed. As we consider our future, many knowledgeable people wonder who will provide the services and perform the installations and construction that support our very society daily. The increasing need for plumbers, electricians, carpenters, brick masons, chimney sweeps, landscapers and so many others has created a business environment where employers are having to either give up on their dreams of expansion, or deal with the demands of a work force that wants more and more of the monetary return of the business. Today's employee is placing an increased demand for higher benefits and higher compensation on their employer.

The problem is further magnified by the overriding cry by educators and politicians that our children must attend college to be successful in life. Many times, they are not even looking at the growing demand for blue-collar skills and how to build these skills through trade schools, technical training, apprenticeships, even on-the-job training.

The COVID pandemic of 2020 has changed our world forever; many businesses have not survived, and this has resulted in a world where many workers will require retraining and the acquisition of new skills as they move into new career paths. But this transition requires that business and industries step up to the plate with new processes for onboarding and training to make this transition successful.

Today we have a tremendous skills gap that affects so many companies and, in fact, cripples their growth and success as they cannot find the new hires they need. To move forward, they must find ways to identify the basic skills level of their new recruits and determine how to build on those skills. Adding further to this is the diversity of learning styles of the workers we hire. How do we train through the different learning styles and communicate effectively with the different generations? This diversity of learning styles and generational differences has produced a society of multiple forms of American culture throughout our country.

So, this book is needed in today's technology equipped world; employers need to make "all-star workers" of today's high school graduate, who frequently lack the basic skills required by today's employers. Often, an employer will say he needs applicants that know which end of the hammer to hold. It is amazing how many prospects cannot read a tape measure or know the difference between a pair of pliers and a set of vice grips. This sad fact is now a major challenge for employers, commonly called the "skills gap." One must fully realize that there is a skills gap between what the new hire may bring with them with their background and the desire of the employer to have a highly skilled workforce.

The problem can be blamed on many factors; one is the increasing number of children who are born and raised in a fatherless or one parent home. There is also the change of the skill level that can be traced to the differences between the generations and what children once did to utilize their spare time, compared to a child of the modern era. Older generations likely, as children, built treehouses, using basic skills, while today the emerging workforce grew up playing with Game Boys, Play Stations, and other electronic devices and gained computer skills in grade school.

Today, the workshop behind the home or in the basement, once a feature of many homes in America, is no longer there. Many children of an earlier age were trained by their fathers to work with their hands. To top this off, many of the chores around the home that at one time the child performed as a part of their upbringing are now contracted out, such as mowing, painting, and general home repair. There has been a radical departure from previous generations, such that the word "chores" is simply not a part of parenting in an average home. Nor is the practice of an allowance that provided payment to the child when they completed their household work assignments.

There is also a glaring lack of vocational training in today's high schools. A very close friend of mine in the Charlotte NC area has started a programs he calls "Tools in Schools" that is putting work tools in the hands of students, many of which they have never seen before or understand how to use. We are not talking complicated tools; rather, we are talking normal hand tools. The current educational thinking is that today's child must be equipped to take their SAT test and prepare for a college education, that will likely drive them to a college where they earn a degree that may or may not bring them a sellable skill.

Quite frankly, the present thought process of many American parents is that their children must go to college, and few envision them being a plumber, carpenter, HVAC technician or any other type of blue-collar worker.

All of this has settled today's society into a position where a lack of basic knowledge, gained during our childhood, can be utilized in later life. Our children lack the basic mechanical skills that would be the starting point to learn a valued trade in the world of blue-collar employment.

This book was written to establish a process to move forward by equipping businesses with a qualified workforce that has the appropriate skills and culture to do the job properly and in a way that will build profit for the company. The goal is to provide strategies that a business owner/manager can use to train the new emerging workforce to be productive and profitable members of their team.

As the author of this book, my goal to establish a baseline for employers to build a system that works in today's world, across different generations and a variety of learning styles. I firmly believe there is an answer; the answer will lie in a change in the way we recruit, the way we onboard, and the way we train. Unless the company of today makes the changes required to thrive in the future, instead of being a picture of success, may well be a painting of failure.

Change is painful, and people have a hard time with it due to the pain of the change. Only after one has decided that the pain of change is easier to tolerate than the pain they are enduring by maintaining the status quo will change become commonplace. The intent of this book is to provide a path for the change required that will produce the results that we all are searching for.

CHAPTER SUMMARY:

- The supply of blue-collar workers has not kept up with demand
- Over-emphasis on traditional 4-year college as the "only" accepted path has worsened the problem
- Due to this, businesses cannot grow in the way their owners envision
- The COVID pandemic has had a tremendous impact on our economy, with many businesses closing their doors, often forever
- These closures mean there are many people in the workforce who will need to gain new skills to become employable
- There is a large gap in basic mechanical and tool skills between past and current generations
- We will need to train our employees – they will not come to us with the skills we need

JERRY ISENHOUR

NOTES

Question: _____

_____

Question: _____

_____

Question: _____

_____

_____
_____
_____
_____
_____
_____
_____
_____
_____
_____
_____
_____
_____

JERRY ISENHOUR

THE BLUE-COLLAR-WORKER/SKILLED TRADES WORKER

―――― ◆◇◆ ――――

When we use the term blue collar worker, what is the origin and why are they called blue collar? A blue-collar worker is a working-class person who performs various types of non-agricultural manual labor. Blue-collar work may involve skilled or unskilled labor in manufacturing, mining, sanitation, custodial work, oil field work, construction, mechanics, maintenance, warehousing, firefighting, technical installation, and many other types of physical work. Often something is physically being built, assembled, or maintained. These jobs are found in residential, commercial, and industrial business ventures. Blue collar workers commonly get their hands dirty, wearing gloves and other protective clothing to keep clean, but also as a safety measure. One of the realities of blue-collar work is that there is often risk and danger involved in completing tasks, and therefore one of the most important aspects of training is to pass along the guidelines that are required to provide for the safety of the worker.

Blue-collar work is most often compensated with hourly pay, though there are also companies that will have compensation plans based on performance, commonly called commission. There is a wide range of pay scales for such work, depending upon field of specialty and experience. At times blue-collar work will also involve customer service and sales roles that the worker must fill, hence the need for varied skills to ensure success in the position.

The term blue-collar itself stems from the image of manual workers wearing blue denim or chambray shirts as part of their uniforms. Industrial and manual workers often wear durable clothing that may be soiled during their work periods. Darker colors conceal dirt or grease on the worker's clothing, helping him or her to appear cleaner. Some blue-collar workers have uniforms which promote the name of the business, and the uniform is often a part of the company branding, image, and marketing.

Historically, the popularity of the darker colors among manual laborers contrasts with the popularity of white shirts worn by people in office environments and has served to enhance the blue collar/white collar dichotomy with socio-economic class connotations. However, this distinction has become blurred with the increasing importance of skilled labor, paying high wages, and the growth in low-paying white-collar jobs. In today's world, the earnings of the blue-collar worker often will exceed the earnings of the white-collar worker.

As one views the relationship of the white-collar worker to the blue-collar worker, there can be a disenfranchisement of one side to the other, where one does not recognize the value of the other. Perhaps this is seated in the view that blue-collar work is "lower class", and white collar is "higher class". When we speak of white-collar, this is often the person in a supervisory role who oversees and directs the blue-collar worker, which can cause a lack of respect and reduces the sense of value with which one views the others on the team.

To the management level person reading this book, or the person assembling the training, a part of your own training must be in leadership style. Your leadership style and skills will determine whether you will have success or failure in your endeavors.

There are three facets of success you must master as a manager or leader of others in order to succeed in today's world. They are:

- Leadership
- Culture
- Systems

There are three skills you must have, and continuously work on, to take your team to the highest level. They are:

- Communication
- Understanding
- Action

So even though this book is about training your team members, it is of the utmost importance that you embark on a program of growth of your own leadership skills, and through this build your communication skills, your ability to understand others, and what you can to ensure they better understand you. Also, realize that others will view your actions or lack of actions as the true test of your leadership skills.

Unless workers have a leader, who leads by persuasion, not by force, there will be failure. The workforce of 2020 does not follow a leader who utilizes force and fear, rather they follow a leader who is charismatic and can lead by their words and actions through persuasion.

CHAPTER SUMMARY:

- "Blue collar" refers to people who perform non-agricultural manual labor
- These jobs often involve risk or danger, making proper training even more important
- "White collar" jobs are often managerial or supervisory, and this can create disenfranchisement between blue and white collar workers
- You, as the manager or trainer, must be aware of and continually work on your leadership skills
- Your employees will judge your leadership skills by what they see you do
- Leading by force or fear will not work. People need to want to follow you

NOTES

Question: _____

_____

Question: _____

_____

Question: _____

_____

JERRY ISENHOUR

UNDERSTANDING THE GENERATION GAP

One of the challenges in training a recruit will be hiring a person who is of a different generation than the person managing or training them. Often managers and trainers face failure simply due to a difference in the generations, their speech, and mannerisms. The effective trainer must endeavor to listen to those from other generations, always keeping in mind how the generations differ, develop methods of communication that all generations understand, and speak in such a way that all generations get it and buy into it. As society changes and evolves, this becomes a more and more difficult task, but success on your part will require a concerted effort to command this communication skill.

One of the leading skills of the trainer / manager is their ability to listen - listen to understand, not to form replies. Once one learns the skill of listening to understand, the words they reply with will come across as persuasion, not as demand. The word "I" is a word less seldom used and the word "we" becomes much more commonly used.

To assemble and implement a training program that works in today's world, it is imperative that each person administering the program understand that a working knowledge of the difference between the various generations is important. Without this understanding, a viable training program cannot be assembled that will accomplish the goals of the program. As we go through the generations, you must recognize which you, and your new hires, are a part of, as the program must be established and built to work with the generation or generations you are hiring, and you must be able to recognize and acknowledge your own generational thoughts.

As such, developing a working knowledge of the differences in generational thinking is a required skill if you are to design, implement, and/or administer a training program for your company. The time spent in gaining this understanding will pay huge dividends in your success strategy. As you delve into the generational differences, pay close attention to the generation of which you are a member.

At the time this book was written, the generations had been classified into four categories:

- ❖ The Baby Boomer – born between the mid-1940's and mid-1960's
- ❖ Generation X – born between the mid-1960's and 1980
- ❖ The Millennial – born between 1981 and the mid-1990's
- ❖ Generation Z – born between the mid-1990's and the early 2010's

-The Baby Boomer Generation (ages - mid-50's to mid-70's in 2020)

The Baby Boomer is a person who was born in the period from the mid-1940s to mid-1960's. As a group, baby boomers were the wealthiest, most active, and most physically fit generation up to the time they arrived. They were the first to grow up genuinely expecting the world to improve with time. They were also the generation that received peak levels of income; they could, therefore, reap the benefits of abundant income and choices of food, apparel, retirement programs, and sometimes even "midlife crisis" products. The increased consumerism of this generation has been regularly criticized as excessive. This group grew up in a period of the cold war, the Cuban missile crisis, a presidential assassination, the Vietnam War, the military draft, and a presidential resignation from office. They were also a generation that in childhood was exposed to rioting and anti-war protests. They were the first generation exposed to television, and the first to experience the ease of information exchange through evening news programs broadcasting world events in audio and video. They saw wartime battlefields on their televisions and watched assassinations of public figures live or within minutes of it happening.

-Generation X (ages - 40 to mid-50's in 2020)

Born in a time frame of the mid-1960s to 1980, Generation X is described by researchers as the "latchkey generation". This is due to reduced adult supervision compared to previous generations, a result of increasing divorce rates and increased maternal participation in the workforce, before the widespread availability of childcare options outside of the home. More of their mothers entered the workforce. As adolescents and young adults, they were dubbed the "MTV Generation" and characterized as slackers, cynical and disaffected. In midlife, research describes Generation X adults as active, happy, and achieving a work-life balance. This generation has been credited with entrepreneurial tendencies, and many have moved to high levels in the world of leadership of companies and governments.

-The Millennial Generation (ages - mid-20's to 40 in 2020)

The generation born between 1981 and the mid 1990's are the Millennials. The *Journal of Business and Psychology* finds that Millennials "expect close relationships and frequent feedback from supervisors" to be a main point of difference from previous generations. Multiple studies note that Millennials associate job satisfaction with the free flow of information, strong connectivity to supervisors, and more immediate feedback. Emory University researchers argue that a lot of these traits can be linked to Millennials entering the educational system on the cusp of academic reform, which created a much more structured educational system. Some argue that these reforms, such as the No Child Left Behind Act, influenced this mindset, as many scholars see this as the beginning of the "participation trophy" thought process. Millennials have increasingly sought the aid of mentors and advisers, leading to 66% of Millennials seeking a flat work environment (less separation between the top level and the lower level of workers, less supervision). Researchers also stress the growing importance of work-life balance. Studies show nearly one-third of student's top priority is to "balance personal and professional life." Many studies show nearly 9 out of 10 Millennials place importance on work-life balance, with additional surveys demonstrating that they favor family over corporate values. Studies also show a preference for work-life balance, which contrasts with the Baby Boomers' work-centric attitude. This is likely a generation that viewed values as being driven not by the amount of money earned, but rather by the quality of their personal lives.

The most serious communication disconnect commonly existing today is the disconnect between the Millennials and the Baby Boomers and Generation X. This often due to the lack of understanding of the values and goals of one generation by another. But this is not new;

this was noted in the 1950s and beyond, with a common statement being "What is the world coming to?". The way the world is changing is not bad; rather, it is a lack of acceptance of the change that creates division and conflict. Do we all remember when we were growing up and our parents could not understand us? As such it must be a part of the job skill of the trainer to understand all the generations they will work with.

-Generation Z (ages - young teens to mid-20's in 2020)

Born in the years from the mid-1990s to the early 2010's is Generation Z, the group presently graduating from high school and college and entering the work force. Most employers have not dealt with training them, except for companies that hire teenagers and recent college graduates. This generation has been described as the "the Internet generation," as it is the first generation to have been born after the popularization of the Internet. In Japan, the cohort is described as "Neo-Digital Natives," a step beyond the previous cohort described as "Digital Natives." Digital Natives primarily communicate by text or voice, while neo-digital natives use video or movies. This emphasizes the shift from PC to mobile and text to video among the neo-digital population. The proliferation of the handheld device is a part of this generation, with many of them being provided their own devices at an early grade school level, thus exposing them to the most rapid delivery of information in history at a young age. This generation has also witnessed tremendous growth in the use of artificial intelligence with the most rapid rise in technology in our history and, conversely, seen the drop of printed newspapers and even books, with many print media now being distributed via electronic means.

Effective leaders and trainers must understand each of the generations and, along with this, understand the different mindsets and culture each has been reared in and now possesses, deeply rooted in their minds. In simple terms, the trainer must be able to think like the person they are training. If they are unable to do this, training will be less effective as there will be a communication failure.

One also must realize and start to assemble the strategies to properly manage both the present and future workforce. Statistics show that there will be a marked increase in workplace participation from the Millennial generation, as the following statistics on workforce age show. Along with this, the manager must also begin to prepare for the Generation Z workforce which just now entering the workforce.

The following are the breakdowns of the percentages of each generation in the year 2018:

Baby Boomers: 77,000,000 (seventy-seven million) men and women, many of whom are now leaving the workforce. The percentage of workers in the Baby Boomer generation is estimated at 29%, and this number is dropping due to retirement and death. However, many are staying in the work force longer to delay filing for social security benefits in order to attain a higher monthly return, but also because they lack the savings needed for retirement.

Generation X: 65,000,000 (sixty-five million), many of which will start to leave the workforce in the coming two decades. Some estimates place the percentage of Generation X in the workforce at 60%.

Millennial: 83,000,000 (eighty-three million), the majority of which are in the workforce. This is the largest segment of the workforce of today.

Generation Z started entering the workforce in 2015.

As the statistics show, your available workforce in the coming years will be composed primarily of Millennials and Generation Z; business success will require you to learn to work with these generations, not only as your employees and co-workers but also as your customers. Managers and trainers must effectively communicate with, understand, and create actions that will work with these different generations if success in training is to be a reality.

CHAPTER SUMMARY:

- In order to lead, you must understand the differences between generations in your work force

- Listening to understand, not just to respond, is essential

- Your training program and materials need to take these differences into account

- Knowing your own generational viewpoint will allow you to communicate effectively

- Know the differences between Baby Boomers, Generation X, Millennials, and Generation Z

- The workforce in the coming years will be increasingly made up of Millennials and Gen Z

JERRY ISENHOUR

NOTES

Question: _____
_____

Question: _____
_____

Question: _____
_____

_____
_____
_____
_____
_____
_____
_____
_____
_____
_____
_____
_____
_____
_____

JERRY ISENHOUR

UNDERSTAND THE VARIOUS LEARNING STYLES

To be a great trainer and to develop training programs that work and produce the desired results, your training must include methods to speak to and communicate with the full range of learning styles and be suitable for the workforce to whom you want to appeal. In the past, learning styles were broken down as follows:

1. Visual learning
2. Auditory learning
3. Read/write learning
4. Kinesthetic learning

There is now a more detailed way of approaching learning styles, described by researchers and psychologists as seven personality styles:

- Visual
- Verbal
- Logical
- Auditory
- Social
- Physical
- Solitary

-Visual

People who learn by this method assimilate more with the use of pictures, images, diagrams, colors, and mind maps. They are the people that do not forget the diameter of a steel pipe that was presented in a power point presentation in the form of a well-labeled diagram.

-Verbal

The verbal learner is someone who prefers using words, both in speech and in writing, to assist in their learning. They make the most of word-based techniques, scripting, and reading content aloud. So, for that diameter of the steel pipe I was talking about, they would prefer you write out the full details in the form of a script or memorandum.

-Logical

These are people who prefer using logic, reasoning, and "systems" to explain or understand concepts. They aim to understand the reasons behind the learning and have a good ability to understand the bigger picture. These people would probably demand to see both the visual and the written illustration of the steel pipe I mentioned earlier. After that, they would study it further to make sure that even if none of the information is available when they are installing the pipe, they could deduce the correct dimensions of the steel pipe needed and carry on with the installation process.

-Auditory

These are the category of people who prefer using sound (obviously): rhythms, music, recordings, clever rhymes, and so on, to learn new things. These people are more effective when they hear instructions out loud; auditory learners prefer discussion over written instructions. They, therefore, tend to have stronger communication and social skills. If an employee like this is an engineer, he/she can easily decipher customer requests and translate them into actual engineering tasks.

-Social

These people are the ones who enjoy learning in groups and aim to work with others as much as possible. This set of people can work alone without a problem, but they are at their best when they work with other people doing similar jobs. This way they can easily learn from their collegues, and they remember work processes just by remembering the moment a work mate did a certain thing, or when a joke was told, or that the hammer fell after a certain process was completed.

-Physical

These are the "learn by doing" people who use their body to assist in their learning. Drawing diagrams, using physical objects, or role-playing are all strategies of the physical learner. With these people, you could use all the visual cues in the world, explain to them verbally, and write out the full steps involved in the operation that they are to carry out, but they still would not get it. They learn better when they have been put through the process. Therefore, they are the hands-on approach kind of people. This is usually common when the workers have poor verbal competence and lack a good understanding of visual aids, but many well-educated workers fall into this category.

-Solitary / Intrapersonal

The solitary learner prefers to learn alone and through self-study. These people prefer to work on problems by retreating to somewhere quiet and working through the possible solutions. The downside with these people is the fact that they spend so much time trying to solve a problem on their own, when could have taken it to someone to solve with or for them.

People like park rangers, researchers, and security guards usually have a good solitary learning style.

The truth is that everyone falls into each of these categories to some extent, depending on the learning process that is taking place. It is necessary, therefore, that all these categories be considered when designing a training process, or even drawing up a job description for your staff. Your written and spoken words must encompass each of these categories to achieve the highest degree of success.

CHAPTER SUMMARY:

- Traditionally, learning styles were defined as Visual, Auditory, Read/Write, and Kinesthetic
- Personality styles can be used to determine the best ways to train individuals. These are Visual, Verbal, Logical, Auditory, Social, Physical, and Solitary/Intrapersonal
- Most people are a combination of several types

NOTES

Question: _____

_____

Question: _____

_____

Question: _____

_____

JERRY ISENHOUR

ADDITIONAL PERSONALITY TYPES COMMONLY FOUND IN THE WORKPLACE

---◆◇◆---

As a trainer, it is imperative that you reach the learning and personality styles of everyone you are training, which can be a very challenging and difficult task. As such, I advise you to research each of these thoroughly to become expert in building a training program that takes all these styles and personality types into account. But it delves even deeper, as within these categories one will encounter 'subgroups' or other personality facets that must be accounted for during the training process.

These different personality subgroups, which are also known as temperaments, are significant factors that also affect the learning styles and process of your staff.

These are described below, and divided into two main categories which are:

1. **Extroversion**: Extroverts need social time to get energized. Extroversion reflects the degree to which people like to be the center of attention in social situations, or the degree to which they want to be 'where the action is'. Extroverts want that spotlight shown on them.

2. **Introversion**: Introverts need quiet time to get energized. They typically shun the spotlight (though they may have many friends and like engaging in smaller interactions).

These are then further subdivided into two forms each:

-Extroversion

- ❖ Choleric/Fire Personality
- ❖ Sanguine/Air Personality

-Introversion

- ❖ Melancholic/Earth personality
- ❖ Phlegmatic/Water personality

Your understanding of these 'subdivisions' of personality traits will enhance your ability to communicate with and train people more effectively and successfully.

-Choleric/Fire personality

The choleric person is quickly and vehemently excited by any impression made; they tend to react immediately; the impression lasts a long time and easily induces new excitement.

The choleric worker likes to be the boss, and most of the time, he/she is. A choleric staff member tends to have a lot of drive, can be aggressive and very difficult to control, but they are usually very good at pushing other members of the staff to carry out a task.

This person has high energy, is direct, impulsive, impatient, and strong-willed.

-Sanguine/Air Personality

The person of sanguine temperament, like the choleric, is quickly and strongly excited by the slightest impression and tends to react immediately, but the impression does not last; rather, it soon fades away. They are usually best at marketing and advertising since they tend to talk non-stop about anything. Depending on what their secondary temperament is, they might function well in the technical field. He/she is usually the spirit of the office, as they always have a joke to tell.

This person is socially active, energetic, likes being outdoors, is highly imaginative, gets discouraged easily, and is funny and mischievous.

-Melancholic/Earth personality

The melancholic individual is, at first, only slightly excited by any impression received; a reaction does not set in at all or only after some time. But the impression remains deeply rooted, especially if new impressions of the same kind are repeated. A melancholic worker tends to be very focused on tasks and tend to finish any task that they start. They are likely to have the highest IQ among the staff. This sort of individual is typically shy and reserved; constant encouragement is usually needed to keep them going.

This individual likes things done correctly, almost demands a routine, likes being by themselves, and is contemplative.

-Phlegmatic/Water personality

The phlegmatic person is only slightly excited by any impression made upon him; he has scarcely any inclination to react, and the impression vanishes quickly. The phlegmatic worker is a person that has lots of feelings, shows love to everyone else and is likely to be a very good leader since they tend to get along with almost everybody. He/she would rarely voluntarily be a leader unless their secondary temperament is choleric, since they are very passive people by nature. A phlegmatic worker would adhere to instructions to the letter and, apart from the melancholic worker, is the best person to perform tasks that require full attention.

This individual likes cooperation, is calm, slow-paced and likes sharing.

The choleric and sanguine temperaments are active, the melancholic and phlegmatic temperaments are passive.

The choleric and sanguine show a strong tendency to action; the melancholic and phlegmatic, on the contrary, are inclined to slow movement.

You as a trainer should know that everyone is a blend of at least two to three personalities, but with one being predominant.

The Training Objective

Your first step in the development of the training strategy is to identify your objective: what are the goals of the program you are designing? This will be the foundation of your training strategy and will guide you as you develop your curriculum. The mission of the effective trainer is to hold these various personality traits in his/her mind during the formation, delivery, and review of the training program. The program must be designed to reach the various generations you are training as well as the personalities of the participants. This is where most training programs simply fail. The ability to speak to multiple personalities and keep them involved and learning is a difficult task and one the trainer must work at to gain competence. Trainers often speak to personalities similar to their own, when in fact the best trainers speak to each of the styles in an effective manner.

The purpose of this book is to share with you the methods I have learned from world-class trainers such as John Maxwell, Jeffrey Gitomer, Larry Winget, Randy Pennington, Damien Mason, Scott McKain and others that I have studied and mentored under during my own career, as well as those whom I have not been privileged to study under directly, such as, Zig Ziglar, but have developed much of my methods by reading their books and watching their tapes. One of the methods key trainers use to learn their trade is to watch others who are phenomenal and inspirational in the way they employ their craft when speaking, writing, and teaching. If one truly wants to rise to the top in their field, one is well served to watch the masters of that field. So it is for trainers and teachers: one must have as their goal being an effective communicator in both the spoken and written word.

When observing phenomenal trainers, keep your focus not on just their words but how they deliver those words: their hand motions, their facial features, the speed with which they deliver their message. Watch how they pause, how they increase and decrease their tempo, and how they use props to emphasize their points. Never be a person who trains using a method I call "slaying by PowerPoint", where you, as the presenter, simply read from a screen. Watch those who are effective and those who are ineffective; see how some ply their trade most successfully, and how others fail. This comes from one important habit; they practice, and they work toward improvement with every presentation. They are so connected to the people they are training that they can switch gears in an instant, always staying ahead of and adapting to their audience. This is a true artisan in the world of training, and being an effective trainer will require your allegiance to building your skills daily and with each presentation.

Very few people can speak in an effective manner, such that when they speak, the learner feels the teacher is speaking to them personally. This is the trainer that, when you sit in their room, makes you feel like they are speaking directly to you; many times, you may even forget that others are in the audience. One of the best at this I have ever seen is a speaker by the name of Bob Beaudine. If you sit in an audience listening to him, you feel as if he is speaking directly to you, even though there are many others around you.

Again, to become an effective trainer, one must learn by watching the greats teach, study their methods, and develop a training style that would appeal to all personalities and learning styles. Knowing how to reach the various people you plan to engage in your training will assist you in meeting this goal. And usually you learn about the personality of different individuals by observing their behavior, both in a group and when alone. To be the best at this, you cannot just watch someone else and imitate them. You must work to develop your own, effective, style.

CHAPTER SUMMARY:

- A training program also needs to take into account 'subsets' within the seven personality types
- Each personality type will include extroverts and introverts
- Extroverts are further defined as choleric/fire personalities, or sanguine/air personalities
- Introverts are further defined as melancholic/earth personalities, or phlegmatic/water personalities
- You must define your training objective, and design the training to take into account the various personality and learning styles
- Great trainers don't rely on just words, their delivery is important
- Watch the best trainers, then develop your own methods. You can't copy another's style

JERRY ISENHOUR

NOTES

Question: _____

_____

Question: _____

_____

Question: _____

JERRY ISENHOUR

RECRUITING PEOPLE WHO CAN BE EFFECTIVE TEAM MEMBERS

───── ◆◇◆ ─────

Even though recruiting is the responsibility of the human resources department in a larger company, in the world of small business, recruitment will often be taken on by the owner, in addition to their other job responsibilities. It is of paramount importance that the hiring process be designed from the start to find people who have a mindset and a basic skill level to mate with the company's goals. Therefore, it is imperative that the person responsible for hiring understands what is needed for a candidate to fill the position. This will relate to the methods by which we select our prospects, such as LinkedIn, Monster, local ads, or word-of-mouth, and even the way we search within these methods. Recruitment is where we locate the best seeds that will grow into the mighty trees we need to create a team of stars who are dedicated to the growth of the team, and not concerned only with their own personal return.

Often in blue-collar work, we have faced recruiting errors due to the process to which we subjected the new person on our team. We take a warm body, invest money to train them, then find out they do not fill the role we really need. Unfortunately, this usually happens after they have been on our team for a period and we have had the ability to observe them at work. To develop a strategy of assembling a team of rock stars, it is imperative that we start by searching the available population for people who match our needs. Otherwise, failure is likely assured, and a loss will occur in that the person will simply not fit in, will not be what we need, and will become a source of frustration. A bad hire or hiring failure can be an expensive loss and can wreak havoc on the business operation. As such, I highly advise that you examine the initial onboarding process you are using to determine if your present system is a liability and not an asset.

As before, think of a new hire as a seed for a great tree. The best trees come from the best seeds; the strongest trees will have the correct background to produce the best fruit when they mature. This is the goal of the hiring process: to find and develop a member of your team that produces great fruit in the form of sales, profits, customer satisfaction - all the things that you desire and your customer searches for when buying your products or services. The recruiting manager must be determined to locate and recruit those who have the right stuff with regards to the company culture and mindset; skills can be taught, but we must also realize which basic skills the recruit possesses and which we must provide in our training process. It is much easier to teach skills than it is to correct flaws in culture and mindset; in fact, it will often be impossible as the die cast in their childhood determines the type of person they are as an adult.

If you don't have a human resources manager, and are filling this role yourself, learn to develop your own process for recruitment marketing. It is destined to become a part of your overall marketing plan, as the hiring of new people will likely turn into an ongoing project in your company. The importance of this cannot be stressed highly enough as you build your team.

Today's world requires more than just placing some ads for your company. Today's prospects want to know about your culture, why you do what you do, how it is good for the world. Understanding your prospect's needs as a member of your team will enable you to reach your dream, the dream of a team of rock-solid rock stars, who will work with you to move your company to a higher level, the level you have dreamed of. A successful recruiting process will require the candidate to know your story, and why the company does what it does.

Recruitment and hiring in today's world will require a marketing plan to seek out prospects, much as the products and services you provide and sell need a marketing program. It will also require that this be a part of your website and social media pages. Production of videos that tell the story of why you are the right place to work, how you can be the start of a new career, and the culture your company offers are all a part of the marketing program you must develop. You are now competing for the good people, and your marketing thrust must present the image that you are the choice employment location for your market area.

All too often business owners are searching for people who are out of work. Changing that thrust to looking for people who are ready for a career change, who are seeking a better way to provide for their families, may well be the right pond for you to be fishing in. This will be like fishing, in that the right bait must be presented in a way that grabs the prospect and directs their attention to your company.

-The interview process A successful team will be built from the people you recruit. Successful recruiting will involve a dedicated strategy, one that includes a well thought out plan for the interview process. As such, the person conducting the interview must understand how use the interview to recruit the right person. Even though this is a manual on how to train, I cannot reinforce strongly enough the need for the right interview process; you are selecting the seeds that will hopefully grow into mighty members of your team. The selection process must include research to determine whether your prospect can survive in the environment in which they will be planted. Therefore, I suggest there be a series of interviews with every prospective team member. Successful hiring strategy includes up to three interviews; the first being a phone interview, followed by two face-to-face interviews.

Sometimes this will include a 4th interview, where the potential team member is taken to a job site to see the type of work done on a daily basis. After all, you do not want to enter into the employment agreement lightly; the work done at this time will be like compounded interest in how it contributes to the success of the applicant and the company.

The hiring interview helps employers and prospective employees learn more about each other and provides the future employee a chance to learn more about the position, while determining whether the relationship will be productive for both parties. Though there are many things you would like to know about a prospective employee before hiring them, you must be cautious about the subject matter you ask about in an interview. Not only are employers prohibited from asking questions that may be interpreted as discriminatory, they should also avoid making statements that misrepresent the requirements and skills required, which will lead to potential employees accepting a job offer based on incorrect assumptions about what the job entails.

The starting point of proper training is the interview process. Without this, you may invest countless dollars and find that success is not realized, and that time and effort is simply lost.

-Pre-employment testing and Assessment

Many successful companies are now utilizing pre-employment testing as a part of their interview process. Two of the most important areas are psychological testing and mechanical aptitude testing. Testing, in a variety of forms and types, has long been recognized by the military as part of their recruitment process. You can test for other basic skills, such as math, to insure the person is prepared to perform the tasks that will be assigned to them.

A number of companies offer this type of testing. It's suggested that you research the various testing processes available to you; many of these have been written by psychometricians after studying the job needs. You can even write your own if you cannot find a set program that works for your business model and your job requirements.

It is also suggested that you consider two additional types of assessment: the DISC Assessment and the Color Code Assessment. Administering these and getting an opinion from a DISC and Color Code Certified Assessor can help you determine whether a candidate has the right behavior patterns to succeed in the position in which you are considering placing them. This can be an additional means of ensuring that you are placing the prospect in the right seat within your organization.

DISC Assessment is a process that detects the behavior patterns of the applicant. The debriefer can then filter through the results to provide an opinion as to whether their behavior and communication style fit both the company and the culture. Utilizing the DISC Assessment process and engaging an expert debriefer can help predict the success or failure of an applicant based on their behavior, communication style, and values.

Color Code Assessment can provide insight into the childhood learning from which a person has developed their behavior patterns. The two assessments together tell you who the applicant is, and how they got the way that they are. Many employers swear by the results of these assessments when making hiring decisions.

You may well feel that you are expending significant effort in the pre-employment process. But, when one realizes the cost of a failure in hiring, the cost and time invested on an assessment is negligible by comparison and proves to be a very valuable resource for you as the manager/trainer.

It must be remembered that the purpose of testing and assessment is to determine if the new hire will be successful. One of the worst, most expensive moves you can make in the hiring process is to hire wrong. As such, developing testing tools as part of the interview and hiring process will be key to determining if the prospective recruit can meet your needs.

CHAPTER SUMMARY:

- Design the hiring process from the start to find people with the desired mindset and willingness to be part of your team

- Learn how to hire the right person, not just the person who's available

- Marketing your business includes marketing to prospective employees

- Hold multiple interviews before making a job offer. The interview process is the start of the training process

- Be clear about the job requirements and expectations, as well as the company culture

- The starting point of proper training is the interview process

- Research and utilize testing programs, or develop your own

- Color Code and DISC assessments provide insight into a person's behavior and early learning, and help determine if they will be a good fit for your team

JERRY ISENHOUR

NOTES

Question: _____

_____

Question: _____

_____

Question: _____

_____

JERRY ISENHOUR

TRAINING

In the history of the trades, training was commonly done on the job. In this process, we take a warm, willing body, put them with someone who is skilled (hopefully) in the job and say, 'now train him'. While this may have worked in the past, we now recognize that this process is very hit-or-miss, to the point that it is highly likely to fail in today's world and should not be relied on, as the need for properly presented training is more important than ever.

There has been vocational training in high schools and community colleges for some trades, but these are limited and, for many trades, they simply do not exist. But we also have the problem of high school guidance counselors believing it is their role to prepare all students for a college education, even when college may not be the ideal destination for a student for any number of reasons. As such, young people are often entering the workforce ill-prepared for the training needed for their profession.

After a person has been employed for a period of time, they may be sent to a training class of some type. This will impart some knowledge, but again it is not usually designed to provide the base skills the person needs to be successful from day one, that put them on a path to the level we desire.

One of the most noteworthy quotes I can provide you is from one of my coaches, Scott McKain. He stated the following, which I feel is a gold nugget; "training is not an event, it is a process". I feel this is truly the approach that the manager and trainer must understand. Training is not a one-time event; rather, training is something for which a process must be developed, and it must be continuous and ongoing. This is one of the reasons why, in my coaching and training practice, I advise a short training each workday - a micro-course of less than 7 minutes. This is a very effective way to add training to our daily regiment, similar to Japanese workers engaged in daily calisthenics, as was seen in the Michael Keaton movie *Gung Ho*.

Training will, at times, also involve retraining, which is harder than training. Retraining involves having to break improper work habits and change the workday routine to which a person has become accustomed, and which many times will fail. In my own career as a trainer, I have found it is easier to train, and much harder to retrain. This is often the case when one hires an experienced worker. They may bring with them the basic skills we need, but they also often bring bad habits, even a bad culture. Again, at some point we suffer a failure, as the person quits, we terminate them, or they stay and become a larger and larger problem for us as an employer and manager. As such, being able to train rapidly is all-important in the optimization of each of our new hires.

Training is a learning process that involves acquisition of knowledge, sharpening of skills, changes of attitude or behavior, adoption of concepts, and learning rules that enhance the performance of the employee and, therefore, make him/her capable of carrying out their expected duties effectively.

Training is not just a one-time thing that is done at the start of employment and then expected to last a lifetime (though I know you probably wish this was the case). Training requires a continuous process that involves every member of both the management and technical teams.

For the training of employees to be effective, certain things need to be put in place. Training involves hiring the right person in the first place and it involves a well-written job description, because the truth is you cannot train a person properly if you don't know the purpose for which you are training them. Effective training requires written standard operating procedures (covered in more detail below) for the tasks that are a part of the job, which guides the trainer on what to focus on in the training. From this comes the initial training protocol as well as all the other forms of training that will be needed for the job. For this to be successful, the trainer must have the required procedures in place to assure a transition from raw recruit to a profitable long-term member of the team.

-Company Policies/Job description/the position agreement

COMPANY POLICIES

In order to ensure that your new hire will successfully integrate into your company's culture, it is imperative that you have written company policies, in the form of an employee handbook. This document should cover your expectations and policies in such areas as attendance, dress code, appropriate behavior on the job, time off (vacation, holiday, and sick time), and use of company equipment and materials. Another area to be covered is substance use. This can be a controversial topic, and in order to avoid any misunderstanding or miscommunication, your expectations in this area need to be covered in detail.

SUBSTANCE USE POLICY

As stated above, one of the areas that must be addressed in your company's rules and regulations is the use and abuse of various drugs. Your business must have clear policy on the use of not only illegal drugs, but legal ones as well: (1) tobacco, (2) alcohol, and (3) marijuana.

Having clear company policy regarding substance use is critical. It should include expectations regarding on-the-job use and should spell out the consequences for violation of the policy. It is up to you, the employer, to decide what policies you will enact for your company, but whatever you decide needs to be written into your employee handbook so there is no misunderstanding.

Tobacco is a drug that was once commonly accepted in our society; however, the acceptance of its use has dwindled severely over the past decades. As an employer, you can disallow the use of tobacco on any job sites, in company vehicles, and/or on any company property. This is a decision that you have the right, as the employer, to make. Some companies, in fact, will not even consider the hire of a person who uses tobacco. This is an extremely sensitive area, as 29 states afford protection for workers who smoke in their off-duty times.

While smokers are not a protected class under federal anti-discrimination laws, state law varies. Employers considering implementing a ban on hiring smokers should carefully review the statutes that apply to their workforce and seek legal counsel, if needed, as there are significant differences between statutes from state to state.

Alcohol is a drug that is legally allowed to be sold in most areas of the country, and legal to consume for anyone over the age of 21. An employer can and certainly should ban the use of alcohol during working hours, and there should be a clear policy that addresses alcohol use outside of working hours, should it affect on-the-job performance. But to deny employment to someone who drinks alcohol during their off-duty hours may be stepping over the line.

Employers can discipline employees for performance or conduct, up to and including termination, even if the employee claims the performance or conduct was due to alcoholism. Again, clearly outlining expectations in your company policy, and stating the consequences for violations of the policy, will go a long way towards preventing misunderstanding down the road.

Marijuana can now be legally purchased in many states; in some states it is only available for medical reasons but in others it can be obtained for recreational purposes. Employers must address this in their policies so there is a clear-cut expectation.

In states where employment is "at-will," meaning companies can dismiss workers without a "just cause," firms likely can prohibit marijuana consumption regardless of state or federal law. Some states are also providing "outs" for employers. For example, California's Proposition 64, which legalized recreational marijuana use, says California employers can penalize workers who test positive for marijuana use, whether or not they were actually high on the job.

Furthermore, with marijuana use of any kind still illegal at the federal level, employees of federal agencies, as well as workers in federally regulated industries, such as transportation, banking, and health care, are prohibited from using marijuana—even during off-hours. If your company performs work for a state or federal agency, you are also responsible for knowing how this impacts the substance use policies of your company. Employers outside of federally regulated industries should stay abreast of changes in state laws, including drug usage and testing laws.

All employers need to keep current on both state and federal laws concerning the use of recreational drugs, and company policy should be revised, as needed, to keep up with any legal changes.

JOB DESCRIPTION

How can you expect someone to fill a job if the duties of that job have not been adequately detailed and your goals for that person clearly defined? First, you need to write a description of the role and what your expectations are. If you do not have the position agreement in place then success will not be found, unless you are extremely lucky. But do you want to build your team and your business on the luck of the roulette wheel? Most likely that answer is no.

You see, that is the beginning of the problem: an employee cannot meet our expectations if we never really shared those expectations in a meaningful way, a way that they can understand. With the increase in the number of millennials in the work force, this is an even more important factor. The generation just entering the work force is one that has to understand the 'why' of what we are doing. You may have grown up as a part of a generation that simply did it because we were told to. The generation that we now must train likely do not understand this as it was not the way they were educated or trained. They came from a generation that was simply expected to participate and not expected to excel. Disagree if you will, but this is traced to the "No Child Left Behind" act signed by the President and further influenced by the "participation trophy" mindset. But you must remember, it is not their fault; society and the present educational system built this generation. Now it is your role, as the leader and trainer, to make members of this generation fit into your operation and business model in a successful manner. In other words, we built this generation, and the failure is ours due to the environment we let encircle them.

A needed part of the recruitment, hiring, and training process is a position agreement that thoroughly details the job role, duties, and expectations. As the leader, you must set up a system of inspection that reinforces and supports what you expect. One of the things that this younger generation requires is constant reinforcement to assure them that they are moving in the right direction. You need to come up with a system of reward, as this is what is expected in today's world. A part of being the manager or trainer is that now, instead of simply managing, one must be a coach, and we can only coach those who are coachable. Part of the interview process is to ensure that all our hires are fully coachable, and are able to learn the skills we need them to have. Without this, the transition to profitable team member will be one that has a multitude of challenges.

CHAPTER SUMMARY:

- On-the-job training, while once the norm, should not be relied on in today's world
- Recognize that many potential employees will come to you without the necessary skills
- "Training is not an event, it is a process"
- Retraining is often more difficult than training
- Training starts with having a thorough job description, including standard operating procedures, as well as written company policies, in the form of an employee handbook
- Company policies should include, among other things, your substance use policies
- A position agreement clearly outlines the job role, duties, and expectations

NOTES

Question: _____

_____

Question: _____

_____

Question: _____

JERRY ISENHOUR

STANDARD OPERATING PROCEDURES

———— ◆◇◆ ————

Your new employee should now know what role he/she must play in your company. In the world in which we live today there is a lot of benefit to paying attention to details. In order to achieve this, there needs to be a standard method that all employees follow when performing a task. Most factories, industries, and workshops have rules, conditions, and procedures that must be followed to make sure that all of the company's product meets a certain standard; this also ensures that the production or work process can be easily supervised, inspected and studied for review.

This, therefore, brings up the need for a Standard Operating Procedure (SOP). An SOP is a set of step-by-step instructions compiled by an organization to help workers carry out operations, from the complex to the routine. SOPs aim to achieve efficiency, quality output, and uniformity of performance while reducing miscommunication and failure to comply with industry regulations. SOPs are also useful tools to communicate important policies, regulations, and best practices.

There are a thousand different ways that a worker could choose to build a product or provide a service for a customer. With an SOP in place, there would be consistency in the final products built by two different workers; this would save money, time, energy and lead to a product line-up that is reliable and delivers customer satisfaction. This is all important in this day and age. It also cuts waste tremendously. Without the structure of the SOPs, your role as trainer will be one that will forever be difficult to navigate successfully.

The SOP is not just a hymn song that workers recite every morning before they begin work (though I see how that can appeal to some people). It is written down, on paper or in digital form, as a formal document. The SOP could be made into a media file and kept online so it is easily available to the workers. Nobody has a perfect memory and can recall every little detail every time, especially when so many complex steps are involved. Therefore, the SOPs are written or made into any form that is easily accessible by the employee, and it is usually made available at the location where the work is carried out. This, therefore, aids the employee when carrying out company jobs. It also helps to keep the training of the worker fresh.

SOPs are useful for every process and operation of the company. They specify every aspect of the company operation down to the minute details. These guidelines will serve as a resource for all members of the team. It will be amazing how having these guidelines help and support a team and how few or no questions will need to be asked – the SOPs contain the answers.

SOPs are also critical when something goes wrong in any part of the process. The answer to how it happened will be one of these statements:

- There is no SOP
- The SOP is wrong
- Someone did not follow the SOP

-Writing Standard Operating Procedures

To achieve the purpose of the SOP, there needs to be one in the first place (obviously). This involves the participation of a person that understands the process intended; the steps should be written down in the simplest form possible, such that every type of worker, regardless of the learning process and personality traits, would be able to easily follow the steps with little or no external assistance. The SOP should also include any potential difficulty that the user may face, as well as information that an inexperienced person will need and can follow.

When writing SOPs, it is important to use clear and easy-to-understand language. Depending on the process involved, the use of flow charts and other types of graphical representation is recommended, as this would aid understanding and would appeal to a diverse group of workers with their different learning styles.

When possible, SOPs should be written in a step-by-step format and utilize a language that emphasizes the importance of compliance, such as 'must,' 'required,' and 'mandatory.'

One of the most important segments of the SOP is the explanation of WHY. This is becoming more and more important as some generations must know the WHY to follow the SOP. If we do not share the WHY, failure should be anticipated.

For assistance, I highly recommend another of my books, *Standardizing Standard Operating Procedures,* which I authored in 2017. In it, I detail my 8-step process that provides a system for writing SOPs that can be understood and followed by team members.

CHAPTER SUMMARY:

- Standardized methods for performing tasks or creating a product ensures standards are met and details are not overlooked
- Standard Operating Procedures (SOPs) are written, step-by-step instructions for carrying out the operations of a company
- If something goes wrong, SOPs can identify the source of the error
- SOPs should be expressed in ways that are understandable to a range of learning styles
- SOPs should include the "why"

NOTES

Question: _____

_____

Question: _____

_____

Question: _____

JERRY ISENHOUR

ONBOARDING (DAY ONE) THE MOST IMPORTANT DAY OF THEIR CAREER

———— ♦◇♦ ————

On Day One, the first task is onboarding, which occurs before the training even begins. The recruit must gain an understanding of the company's mission, how it operates and the role they are expected to play. Company manuals, rules, and regulations must be reviewed. Simply hiring someone and assigning them to a task does not properly prepare them for that task. This part of onboarding may take a half, to possibly a full, day with the person responsible for them in the onboarding process. This may seem like a time-consuming task, but again we are planting the initial seed of success in the new employees' minds. At the end of this onboarding process they should understand your mission and your culture. It is the foundation upon which you will build a valued team of superstars.

But the truth of the matter is that Day One is often a wasted day in the life of many new hires. Most managers completely miss the mark on setting the course of the employee's growth in the company. Let me ask you, what is your present system for Day One? How do you handle the most important day that this person will ever work for you? Do you make this the day that will build their success or will start them on a path of potential failure? Again, Day One is a critical day, likely the most critical day of their employment. Think for a moment back to an earlier time in your life, when you started something completely new; maybe it was your first day in school, kindergarten or first grade. Were you nervous going in? Did your path start then? Did you start to build a relationship with others on that first day? How did these initial relationships play out for you as you moved forward?

At some point in your life, did you go to a new school? Your classmates already knew each other, and you were the new kid; remember how that felt? How did your school career go from that point forward? Well, this is the first day that your new hire will undergo. They are entering a society, an atmosphere that is brand new to them. And likely it has been a crap shoot as to whether they will succeed or fail. Is there a way to make this first day of employment a day that will give them the tools they need to excel for you? I think there is and that is the the concept I want to share with you.

Now I am assuming you have gone through the proper steps in your recruitment process.

You have done the interviews and the pre-employment testing process for personality, mechanical aptitude, math skills, etc. You have properly explained the job role and the company culture, mission, and goals. You have thoroughly explained the expectations you have for this person. If you have not done these steps, then you will likely encounter difficulty. Today is the first day of this business relationship. It is likely that you have already invested time and expense in this person, and now it is time for them to report to work.

So, what is your Day One onboarding process? Does this person simply clock in, and you assign them to someone that is unfamiliar with the proper processes? Or are you now ready to do the work required to make their career one of success? Before going forward, I want to thank one of the members of my team at CVC Success Group, Brandi Biswell, for sharing the processes she uses. She is probably one of the best in this area I have ever had the privilege to work with, and her expertise is much appreciated. Brandi started with me as a client, but once I recognized the expertise she brought to the table, I knew she had to be a member of my coaching and training team.

The first step should be your HR person sitting with this person and reviewing the following:

- The company personnel manual, or employee handbook
- The company SOPs
- Review the expectations again

Once this is done, have them sign off that they have received these, that they understand them, and will follow them.

Yes, that process will take some time, perhaps half of that first day, but isn't that time worth it if you are going to make them successful? It is a part of the investment you are making that will pay huge dividends.

So now what's next? The new team member also needs to gain an understanding of what the company does and what products and services you offer to your customers. Or do you prefer for the recruit to just get this on their own?

You may want to consider onboarding as "organizational socialization". It is the mechanism through which a new employee gains knowledge about the company, the skills to allow him/her to transition into working in the company effectively, and the opportunity to learn more about the culture and values of the company. It is considered by researchers to be one of the most important factors for ensuring that the employee feels motivated to work, and not contemplate thoughts of seeking employment elsewhere, costing you the investment you have expended to recruit and train them.

During the process of onboarding, use delivery methods such as printed text, video orientation, a company tour, and lectures to make the transition of the new member into the organization and their job smooth.

The onboarding process should be about making the new employee feel a sense of welcome, of being valued, a part of a team, and mentally prepared for their role within the company.

CHAPTER SUMMARY:

- Onboarding occurs before training even begins
- This is not "wasted time", it is planting the seeds of success in the new hires' mind
- Spend time reviewing the company handbook and SOPs – then review them again
- Onboarding should make the new hire feel welcome and a part of the team

NOTES

Question: _____

_____

Question: _____

_____

Question: _____

_____

JERRY ISENHOUR

THE TRAINING PROCESS

---◆◇◆---

After the onboarding process of the new employee, he or she goes to work, right? But not so fast: the employee still needs to be involved in some sort of training before starting duty. Even if the employee just came from a similar job, this is still needed.

Which brings me to the next item in this book, the initial training process. In human resource development, this is often referred to as **induction training** and is viewed as a form of introduction for new employees that enables them to perform successfully in a new profession or job role within a business.

Induction training is systematic training, and there should be a strategic plan to ensure success. The systematic model replaces natural learning with an intervention that aligns with the organization's objectives. The features of induction training include:

- ❖ It is part of the organization's overall planning process and is in line with its goals.
- ❖ There is a strategy that shapes the approach to employee development.
- ❖ Skills are planned for and addressed systematically through formal training.

- There is a continuous cycle of training, analysis, activity, and evaluation.

Induction training provides employees with a smooth entry into the organization by providing them with the information they require to get started. The goals of induction training are in line with those of the onboarding process. These goals are to:

- Create a positive atmosphere
- Address new job concerns
- Increase comfort level and feeling of belonging
- Increase knowledge of the organization and its procedures and policies
- Share organizational values
- Share job specific information

In small organizations, the responsibility for carrying out the induction training usually rests with one person. In larger organizations, the responsibility is shared between managers, supervisors, and human resources. In the case of both big and small organizations, the employees and the senior manager play a major role in inducting an employee. Their responsibility is to ensure that the induction program is followed, and the desired goals are achieved. Typically, the human resources department in larger businesses prepares the induction checklist (and updates it periodically), plans and administers the formal program, and assists and advises employees. In smaller companies, these tasks fall on the owner or a senior team member.

The induction itself is usually conducted within the workplace by competent trainers and speakers in a presentation format. Induction training can also be in a written format, which can be sent to a new employee before they start, handed to them when they arrive, or delivered in a computer-based format.

Induction training should result in the new employee being fully integrated into the social organization of the business, with knowledge of the skills and tasks required for their job, and how those skills and tasks fit within its structure. The trainer (or trainers) will know they have accomplished their goals if they observe that the new employee is well integrated into the business' social organization and is prepared to enter the specific area for which they have been trained.

In today's world, much of this training can be provided via a virtual learning platform. This can be an industry specific program that you have access to, or it could be an online learning platform you develop yourself. There is also what I call the hybrid process, where you have access to an industry platform, but you add your own proprietary training sessions. This allows you to fill the specific and proprietary needs of your company, your services, and your products.

-Planning an effective Induction training

The induction is the first real opportunity new employees get to experience and fully understand their new employer, the products they offer, and the services they provide. If, for example, the trainer is substandard or the program lacks the needed depth, new employees may quickly become bored and may even question their choice of employment. Induction training must be comprehensive, collaborative, systematic, and coherent to be effective and make a positive impact with the trainee. Training should include the development of theoretical and practical skills, and be designed to communicate effectively with the new employees, taking into account the learning and personality styles described above.

There are different ways that businesses conduct induction training to enable new staff and recruits to do their work. For example, Starbucks' induction is very practical and clearly sets the expectations of the job; compare that to the Exxon Mobil Graduate program, which spans the first year of employment, with the bulk of the induction training happening in the first two weeks to ensure trainees have adequate background knowledge before receiving job or role training. The right balance of training will include the information necessary for the job, but not be too intensive an information-giving session. If the training is too intensive, it will be ineffective as individuals will start to lose concentration and may end up missing crucial information.

So, after you have assessed the work environment, or you have hired someone do it for you, like a professional trainer, you or they will then choose the best method possible for giving induction training to the new entrants. The professional trainer is usually on a contract basis since they don't work with your company all year long. However, if the company is of sufficient size, then an in-house staff position may be a better option. This will likely be the person charged with designing the training program for the company, making it as effective as possible, and ensuring that it satisfies the staff developmental needs of your company.

We will refer to the initial training going forward as initial basic training, but this all falls under the definition of induction.

CHAPTER SUMMARY:

- The initial training, or induction training, immediately follows the onboarding process

- It is designed to be an introduction into the company, and to enable the new hire to perform successfully in the company and in their position

- Induction training can be done in person, or by using written or electronic means to deliver the information

- Well-designed induction training exposes the new hire to the company culture and expectations in adequate depth, but is not so information-intensive as to be overwhelming

- Assess your work environment, or hire a professional trainer to do so, to determine the best method for presenting the induction training

JERRY ISENHOUR

NOTES

Question: _____

_____

Question: _____

_____

Question: _____

_____

_____

_____

_____

_____

_____

_____

_____

_____

_____

_____

_____

_____

_____

JERRY ISENHOUR

INITIAL BASIC TRAINING

———— ◆ ◇ ◆ ————

To carry forth an effective training program, a strategy for measuring results must be formulated based on daily, weekly, monthly, and quarterly expectations. The trainer should have a set strategy that shows what expectations the new hire will be required to meet, and this must contain the ability to track and measure results, from daily to annual goals. This strategy should cover Day One expectations and lay out the exact time frame for meeting the anticipated results, up to complete knowledge of the position for which the person is being trained. Without this strategy, how will you track and measure the results?

From here we now head to the actual initial training, and this needs to be a classroom setting of some type. It is here that the basics of the job are explained and where the new hire will gain an understanding of the basis of their job.

The following may be a process you have thought of or it may be one that is completely new to you. But I assure you, deep research over many years into what does and does not work was done in the writing of this book. The process is on target, and it will produce phenomenal results. It is the process used by many Fortune 500 companies, and it can work for you if you do the work. This is a process that will require dedication on the part of the trainer and the new hires. You can also train a group using this process, which will further optimize your efforts.

Now as the trainer you will be required to have training aids. There may be online sources for some of this, but as a rule, on-line training or videos often are ineffective unless they are used in a supervised setting. There must be a method of assignment of training, measurement of the training, and assessment of the comprehension of the materials to gauge if the training has been effective.

The question is, what training aids will this process require? Can you obtain these or will you need to produce them? As we talk training aids, this includes the training content. Is there content in your industry that can assist you? Are there education and training suppliers who can assist? Most likely there are.

So, what is the basic knowledge required for the job role they are to fill? This must be determined for the proper strategy to be formulated. My suggestion is that you review this basic information, as well as the tool and mechanical skills, required for the job. This training must cover what will be required to meet and exceed your expectations, and it must cover the why of the tools and the reasons we do the job we do. It must be recognized that many times, as the trainer, you are sharing information you have accumulated over a period of years. It must be presented in a way that your student will understand it, including the terms used and the processes you will follow.

Now, this is where online training can play a big part in the initial training, as there are likely existing programs you can use. But I want to add a word of caution here. An online class will not be successful with many students unless it is done in a monitored and facilitated environment. You may believe you can simply assign these classes to your new hires, and they will learn and move to the highest level. However, this system requires assigning courses, imposing deadlines on their completion, and assessing the results. A system of this type can work, but it must be monitored and constantly inspected to ensure your objectives are being met. Otherwise it is like taking a person to a library and saying, "go in and learn" and never tracking or measuring the results. So, if using a system of this type, monitoring is required by the person entrusted with the oversight of the program.

Content of this type can be used in a group setting very effectively. This gives the additional benefit of interaction between persons being trained, which takes the training to an even higher level.

There are four processes involved in the designing and implementation of your in-house training program:

- ❖ Assessment of Needs
- ❖ Designing Training Material
- ❖ Conducting Training Sessions
- ❖ Tracking and Measuring Results

-Assessment of Needs

This basic training strategy should impart the content required to move the raw recruit into the position of a seasoned veteran in the quickest manner possible. Until you get them properly trained and up to speed, they are often a liability upon which we base future hope. As such, an experienced person who understands the process and the difficulties involved in commanding it should be involved in the training. If that is not you, are there others in the company who can assist in the needs assessment, design of the content, and the presentation? The content must be designed to be understood by the person being trained and take into account their basic skill level. It must also effectively meet the communication needs of the generation you are training.

-Designing Training Materials

Designing training materials and creating content for initial basic training is a critical part of the training process. This is also true for ongoing training. Time spent in the design of the area where training is to take place will pay huge dividends at a later point as this will serve to solidify your offering.

The task of designing and building the content is one of the hardest parts of the entire training process. Designing and writing the content should be done in a way that it is easily understood by the trainee. Poor content will reflect in the benefits of the training being drasically lowered.

There is also the requirement of the presentation setting you will use for your training; will it be a classroom, will it be a hands-on, or perhaps a combination of these? The specific skills for which you are training will be the deciding factor.

In building classroom training, the trainer will likely be required to possess or develop the skills to create and present training programs using PowerPoint, Keynote, or other methods of digital presentation. As a trainer, you will be well served to develop your skills in a variety of presentation formats.

You may also decide to utilize outside sources to develop or deliver the content; most industries have suppliers who do this professionally. Picking outside education courses with content well-suited to your requirements may prove to be a very worthwhile investment. Building content will involve expertise you may possess but likely will require research to assemble the perfect training materials. You will have to invest your time and effort in content development.

As the person responsible for the training, I suggest you do research within your industry and related industries to find content that will be beneficial to your goals and incorporate this into your training materials. Many times, through research, you can locate great materials that you can add to your training content.

You may also need to modify or supplement existing materials. There are books and videos available on many topics, and many times outside experts can provide this for you. If your company has a unique way of doing a common task or a process not widely used by other companies, you might need to write the material yourself. When writing your own training materials, try to break down each task into a few simple steps and organize them by the order in which those steps are usually performed.

It is of the utmost importance, when assembling the training courses, that you remember it must be relatable to the audience. Having materials that do not relate to your audience will produce ineffective results for you. Be sure to design or select training materials that engage the learning styles of your new hires; use text, charts, graphs, audio, and, where possible, hands-on methods to ensure you deliver this information in the way each person learns best.

-Conducting Training Sessions

After you finish designing your training program, you can begin offering it to your team. Training isn't just for new hires -- you must also prepare training for established employees. For instance, you can offer a course on sales techniques to new hires as part of the orientation process, and to experienced salespeople as a refresher course. When conducting the training, go through the steps in your materials in a logical, step-by-step fashion. For instance, in a sales training course, you could cover the techniques for the initial sales contact, followed by techniques for overcoming objections, and then for closing the sale.

But the key for training is the interaction with those you are training. This interaction will allow you to reinforce the concepts offered in ways that allow the student to more readily understand how to adapt this to their own daily processes.

-Tracking and Measuring Results

Always have a clear, measurable, and unambiguous goal for your training courses. For example, a customer service training course could have the goal of increasing the percentage of complaints resolved on the first contact by 10% in the six months following the course. If you set a clear and measurable goal ahead of time, you'll find it much easier to assess whether your training is effective the way it is or needs to be redesigned. As such the tracking of results is of the utmost importance in gauging the value of the training.

-Advantages and Disadvantages of in-house training

In-house training courses aren't the perfect solution for everyone. I have, therefore, decided to highlight the advantages, disadvantages, and considerations of in-house training so you can know if it is the right path for you and your company.

-Advantages versus Disadvantages:

- ❖ **Training cost saving:** The amount spent for training a number of employees is less than if the same number of people were sent out for training, since the resources used in carrying out the training are owned by the company itself, and the cost is the same regardless of the number of people being trained. Conversely, when the training is being done elsewhere, you will usually pay a per-person fee.
- ❖ **Can be presented when you need it:** If one is relying on outside training, they must wait until it comes to an area near them. Sometimes, it simply is not available in the time frame required.
- ❖ **Travel cost saving:** Since the training is done at the company, the cost of transportation and possibly accommodations at the location of the training center is eliminated.
- ❖ **Use of in-house projects for case study scenario:** In-house training means ongoing jobs in the company can be used as real-life examples, which are significantly more effective than generic examples.
- ❖ **Convenience:** Organizing training for a group of individuals, all with their own timetables and responsibilities, can be a

very difficult task. However, by having training courses in your own building, working around people's schedules becomes a lot easier, as you are cutting out logistical issues as well as the fact that candidates can be easily reached in case something arises that needs to be addressed quickly, such as a delay in a trainer arriving or a work emergency that requires "all hands on deck".

- ❖ **Teamwork:** Having staff from different departments come together to achieve a common goal during the training period leads to building a workforce that relies on teamwork, and it fosters a better relationship between all the staff involved. It never hurts to have a workforce that is happy and up to date.

- ❖ **Keeps control of your team:** Sending your team members to a remote location where they can establish relationships with others can have a detrimental effect, as it causes issues brought on by others, such as inappropriate behavior by others that could influence your team. It can also expose your team members to those who are head hunting for great team members.

CHAPTER SUMMARY:

- Effective training requires a strategy for quantifying results and measuring performance

- Initial training should be presented in a well-designed classroom setting

- It should provide new hires with the necessary knowledge and skills to be successful

- Digital or online training can be very useful, but must be used in a supervised setting to be effective and should include deadlines for completion as well as a means of measuring comprehension of the material

- The processes involved in the design and implementation of a training program are assessment of needs, design of the materials, conducting the training, and tracking results

- Design your training materials to reach a variety of learning styles, which can include modifying existing materials to suit your company's needs

- Interactive training allows reinforcement of concepts so they are more readily understood

- There are advantages and disadvantages to in-house training; consider these when deciding if this is the right path for your company

JERRY ISENHOUR

NOTES

Question: _____

_____

Question: _____

_____

Question: _____

_____

JERRY ISENHOUR

OUTSIDE/OFF-SITE TRAINING

───── ♦◇♦ ─────

Off-site training is usually utilized when you have participants coming from multiple locations to attend a training at a common location set up for that purpose. This is often done when the training required cannot be provided by the staff of the company. Also, if the number of employees requiring training is small, then it would be cost ineffective to organize an in-house training for them, as the time and money that would be spent in organizing such training would be greater than the amount that would be spent if they were sent for off-site training.

Off-site training is necessary for your staff if the material can only be taught by the person carrying out the training, by virtue of his/her technical expertise. For instance, suppose there is only one person that knows how to build the new phone that can work as a phone and be used to power a laptop. Then, anyone who wants to learn to make such phones would have to travel to meet the trainer at a location that is set up for the training.

-Selecting and implementing an off-site training

Most, but not all, of the process of selecting and implementing off-site training for your staff is like the process for developing an in-house training program.

There are five processes involved in utilizing an off-site training program:

- ❖ Assessment of needs
- ❖ Search for a suitable training event
- ❖ Arrange the resources needed for the training exercise
- ❖ Plan time off for the training session
- ❖ Assess the results

-Assessment of needs

The design of an effective off-site training program involves researching what area of the present job process would benefit from improvements, the form of training that will most benefit the process, and which members of your staff would gain the most from training. It may be that the type of training program you need is better suited to be presented off-site. Once you determine whether your needs are better met by in-house or off-site training, you can move on to the next step.

-Search for a suitable training event

Unlike the in-house training, you are not the person who will organize the training event. You will, therefore, need to find a suitable training event that meets the requirements of what your staff needs to learn. In some cases, you may even request a training event, by contacting someone who is an expert in the field of what needs to be learned by your staff.

-Arrange the resources needed for the training exercise

After you have successfully secured a training session for the staff members, you must arrange for the resources that will make the training possible.

- ❖ **Transportation -** Since the training is off-site, the first thing to be considered is transportation to and from the event
- ❖ **Accommodations -** The next thing to consider is accommodations for your staff members, if needed. You will have to secure accommodations that are close to the training event and are cost-effective and comfortable for your staff.
- ❖ **Meals -** You may need also to devise a meal plan for your staff. Meals are sometimes provided as a part of the training costs, or you may need to provide a per diem, or daily meal allowance, to the employees attending the training. Either way, you need to make sure this is taken into account when planning the training exercise.

-Plan time off for the training session

The employees being sent to a training session will not be around to do their jobs, so you need to plan time off for them in advance and make sure that someone else is available to do their jobs, unless the job function can be put on hold for the duration of the training.

-Assessing the Results

Just like in the in-house training, you should always have clear, measurable, and unambiguous goals for your training courses. I feel that for off-site training courses, it is easier to actually assess the result and check the improvement in performance. For example, if you send out some of your staff to attend an intensive training on a new process, when they come back you would expect them to be able to perform the process successfully. The performance can be evaluated by how effectively they produce or provide the product, how it performs, and how prone it is to suffer failure or callbacks after completed. Therefore, as part of the preparation process for off-site training, the desired result should be known, both by you and the staff attending the training. As with all training, a plan for tracking and measuring results is imperative.

-Advantages and Disadvantages of an off-site training

Off-site training courses are usually seen as having more disadvantages than advantages, but that is not always the case. It will depend on the attendee's ability to comprehend and the presenter's ability to properly instruct in a meaningful and understandable manner. As I have pointed out, the purpose of attending the training in the first place would determine whether off-site training would offer advantages or disadvantages; only proper training design, setting expectations and measuring the results can provide the answers.

Here are the advantages and disadvantages of off-site training.

-Advantages

- ❖ **Staff morale** – Off-site training can boost the staff morale in your company since they get to travel and meet new people. They also feel valued because the company is willing to make an investment by sending them for off-site training.
- ❖ **Pay attention** - Employees on off-site training tend to pay attention to the training itself, since the only distraction they will have, apart from the great view from the hotel, is the

food. There will be no interruptions by the boss, no picking up of phone calls for the office; they are there for one purpose only, the off-site training. It must be made clear that they are being sent to learn; it is not a vacation nor is it time off.

- ❖ **Engaged** - The activities performed in off-site training should be engaging and professionally designed. The employee would, therefore, get more from and be more engaged by a well thought out and well-presented training by a professional than the one put together by George from Human Resources for an in-house training session.
- ❖ **Networking** - I still think this is the most important feature of off-site training. Of course, you want your staff to learn, that is why you sent them on an all-expense-paid training, but the benefit of meeting new people from different companies can be invaluable to your staff and your company.
- ❖ The internet is popular today because it makes it easy to network across the globe; that is fine, but nothing beats the old fashioned, meeting people one-on-one and just hitting it off from there. During off-site training, your staff gets to see how other people from different companies solve similar problems, and they get to learn new methods of problem-solving. Nothing beats that.
- ❖ **Flexibility** - One of the very cool things about off-site training is the ability of the trainer to say "today, we will learn how to build computers in a swimming pool." My point is that it is very flexible, any effective teaching tool can be used, and it will still be a home run with the points the instructor makes.

- ❖ **Expertise** - If you do the same thing repeatedly, for a long period of time, each time being creative and using different methods, you should become so good you can be called a specialist. This is the same with those that organize off-site training classes; they have done this repeatedly for a very long time, and they are usually professionals or specialists in their respective fields. With this level of expertise, you can be sure you are getting the very best value for your money.

Disadvantages:

- ❖ **Price** - The training centers for off-site training are usually dedicated to doing just that, so, it will cost more than if you run it at your company or office space.
- ❖ **Time off work** - Your staff will have to take time off work for the entire period of the training, meaning you probably will be understaffed for that period.
- ❖ **Travel** - Your staff will have to travel to the location of the training, which will also cost money and will have its own risks.
- ❖ **Recruitment** - You must be aware that a remote training can frequently expose your work force to headhunting by others looking to expand their own staffs.

Consider the advantages and disadvantages of off-site training; take a step back and review what is truly important to your business.

Your staff is one of the most vital elements of the success of your company. Without them, work would not get done, product would not be manufactured, and your business would not be able to keep operating. Therefore, although there are costs associated with training, it's important to make sure your staff has all the skills needed to be able to carry out their work.

CHAPTER SUMMARY:

- Off-site training can be the better choice when the training can't be provided by a member of the staff, or when the number of people being trained is too small to make organizing an in-house training cost-effective

- The process of selecting an off-site training program is similar to what is needed to develop in-house training

- Using off-site training requires research to find the right program, arranging the necessary resources, and facilitating trainees' participation

- Just as with in-house training, there should be clear, measurable, and unambiguous goals

- You need to compare the advantages and disadvantages of in-house and off-site training to determine which is the best course of action

- A well-trained staff is essential to the success of your company

NOTES

Question: _____

_____

Question: _____

_____

Question: _____

_____

JERRY ISENHOUR

CONTRACT TRAINERS

———— ◆◇◆ ————

A contract trainer goes by many definitions, but I will stick to the one I believe communicates the information I am passing along best. A contract trainer is a person who is an expert at evaluating what a company or an organization needs in the form of training and can recommend as well as execute a training plan for the staff of the company. They are not a part of the permanent staff of the company, but rather carry out their duties on contract basis, hence the title "contract trainers".

They will frequently have specialized in the assessment aspects of training as well as designing and presenting programs, but you should look for their experience with similar companies before hiring and check out their track record of success.

Training companies come in all sizes and levels of expertise. Their services range from one-time training on specific or general skills, to providing all the training in the variety of formats your company needs.

Primarily, a trainer is a specialist at training employees in multiple aspects of their area of specialization.

Contract trainers must always have an up-to-date understanding or knowledge of the subject on which they are to train your employees.

These trainers should stay on the forefront of change, keeping up with the events of the industry in which they carry out their training and be qualified to present on a variety of subjects relating to their skills. A contract trainer should be recognized as a subject matter expert in the areas in which they train others.

-Hiring contract trainers

Finding and retaining good people with the right skills to develop training for your employees can be a real challenge, not to mention very costly. Many organizations choose to hire training consultants they need – such as instructional designers or e-learning project managers - on contract, recruiting them for specific projects over set periods of time. This can be a more viable option for various reasons including

- Lower overall costs
- Organization has greater flexibility with consultants
- Less seat time – consultant is only being paid for the work they do

So, what rules should an organization follow to ensure they get a contract training consultant who's right for the job?

- ❖ **Clearly define the role:** Before you even start looking for a contract trainer, you need to have a written expectation of what role you expect them to play in your company. This written document should contain what you expect from them as your contract trainers, and their relationship with your staff should be clearly stated in the written document as well. After the document has been completed, reviewed by your legal representative, and he/she has approved the content, it then becomes a written contract.

- ❖ **Careful selection:** Whenever possible, it is a good idea to take your time when selecting a new contract training staff. You should review and verify their credentials and certifications, along with their educational background; you should interview them to make sure their past experiences and skills match what your company's staff requires for development. The selection process is very important since it determines if your staff will benefit from the training contract or if it will just be a waste of your company's resources and time.

- ❖ **Evaluate their experience:** More accurately put, what is their experience in relation to the type of project you would have them working on? Training projects vary depending on their target audience – for example, the approach to a new hire training program will differ greatly from a compliance training program for senior management, in terms of design, content, and layout. If you are seeking a contract instructional designer, ask yourself, what types of projects and what areas of learning and development do they offer?

- ❖ **Align the roles with their career objectives:** This is quite important and yet it is often overlooked. Even though a training consultant might be working on a contract for a fixed period, they should be viewed as a credible and valued member of the team, and their career goals acknowledged. Where possible, you should try to align the role you are recruiting for with the successful candidate's goals and make them aware that they are regarded as an important member of the team.

Remember, a contract role can often develop into something long term if the trainer demonstrates real ability, so it is worth showing them their efforts are appreciated from the beginning.

❖ **Onboarding makes a difference:** Consider the onboarding needs of your training consultant. In busy times, it is very easy to drop a new project on him or her and leave them to it without providing sufficient information about your needs and expectations. Prior to bringing a training consultant into your company, they must fully understand the organizational culture, participant's learning styles, and the nuances of their role. This should all be included in the onboarding process.

CHAPTER SUMMARY:

- Contract trainers are experts at evaluating training needs and designing appropriate training programs

- Hiring the right contract trainer requires clearly understanding your company's needs and conducting research to find the right fit for those needs

- Making your contract trainer a part of your team includes acknowledging and aligning your needs with their career goals

NOTES

Question: _____

_____

Question: _____

_____

Question: _____

JERRY ISENHOUR

THE CONTINUOUS TRAINING PROCESS

———— ◆◇◆ ————

While many companies invest time, money, and energy on induction training for new employees, they often overlook and fail to understand the importance of continuous training and development for the entire workforce. And this is exactly why many companies fail to maintain their success and experience a high employee turnover rate.

Studies show that 39.3% of job seekers today consider 'growth' to be a distinguishing and a top characteristic when evaluating a new job opportunity. They'd be ready to switch from their current jobs to a new job opportunity if it offered them opportunities to grow and climb the corporate ladder.

Therefore, instead of just focusing on induction courses and mentoring new employees, it is extremely important that your HR department devises continuous training programs for existing employees, and provides them with opportunities to grow, both personally and professionally. Your training programs should be set out according to your organizational needs and (often rapid) industry developments, so that your employees are kept abreast of the changes and have adequate skills to perform their daily tasks efficiently. Your training must also encompass changes in business offerings to meet the needs of your customer base. A company, if they are to be successful for the long haul, must be on a path of ongoing reinvention of the business, its products, the way it markets, and the way it provides its products and services. Companies that do not reinvent themselves as needed are faced with eventual extinction. Compare Sears to Amazon. If Sears had reinvented itself when required, they would almost certainly be Amazon today. But we can all see that Sears drifted into a position of near extinction, while Amazon continues to take over more and more market share wherever they place their attention, often not by beating competitors, but rather by buying them.

As the organization grows and the employees grow with it, the training needs change, and the skills the employees require for success are constantly evolving as well.

Therefore, continuous training is any activity involved in the development of the employee's skill and knowledge, in accordance with the job's requirements as time goes on. Unlike onboarding and induction training, it applies to all employees in the company or organization.

-Benefits of continuous training

Some organizations ignore continuous training sessions for employees as they feel they are expensive, with employees missing work time while attending these sessions, which causes delays in completion of projects. What they fail to grasp are the underlying benefits of these continuous training sessions and how they contribute to the organization in the greater scheme of things! Benefits of conducting these programs are significant and long-lasting. Often a common concern expressed by leadership is the fear of 'what if we train them and they leave'? The other side of that is 'what if we do not train them and they stay'?

Here are some of the benefits of continuous training:

- ❖ **Reduce/address weak links:** A continuous training program allows you to develop and strengthen the skills your employees need or should improve upon. It helps reduce weak links and ensure mistakes are not repeated. It is a great way to address issues in a timely manner and ensure organizational productivity is not compromised.
- ❖ **Improve employee satisfaction:** Access to continuous training programs and workshops shows employees that they are valued. They feel appreciated, challenged, and more satisfied with their jobs. It helps them move up the learning curve and work harder and more effectively.
- ❖ **Boosts employee performance:** Continuous training empowers employees. It gives them the confidence of knowing that they are abreast of new developments and have a stronger understanding of the industry. This confidence pushes them to perform better and think of new ways to excel. Increases in employee performance leads to increases in organizational productivity. A team of competent and knowledgeable employees is all that a company needs to compete successfully and hold a strong position in their industry.

-Designing a continuous ongoing training program

The design of a continuous training program is very similar to any other training scheme that we have talked about in this book. The only difference is the fact that it is continuous; in-house or off-site training can be part of a continuous training program.

So, it involves the same process of design as the training type that is now in use.

It consists of:

- ❖ **Assessing training needs:** Just like any other training method, you need to figure out what your staff lacks in terms of training, on either new or existing production methods. The only way you know if your staff requires new training is if you monitor their working process, and have information on the current working process of other companies using similar methods, or producing similar goods, for comparison. This way you would know if there is a disparity in the method your staff uses and, say, the newest, most efficient method in town.

   Sometimes, the release of a new service or product in the market might be what prompts you to design a training program for your staff.

- ❖ **Choosing a training program:** After you have figured out what type of training your staff requires to improve their performance and production efficiency, you can then decide if you should have them take an off-site training, or an in-house training taught by a contract training staff. Discuss this with your human resources staff to determine which one would best suit the the needs of the staff and the company.

❖ **Assessing the result:** Just like you do with any other training, you need to assess the results. Depending on the training subject matter, you need to find the most suitable method for evaluating your staff's performance, based on the new training. For instance, if they were trained on a new machine, then the best way to assess their performance would be to have them work on the new machine and evaluate their output. If they are trained on a new production process, let them use the new production process for a period of time, then assess whether they have improved output, efficiency, or some other measure.

The assessing of needs and results should be performed regularly to make sure the staff is always performing at peak efficiency.

CHAPTER SUMMARY:

- Training is not just for new hires; it should be continuous
- Ongoing training provides opportunities for employee growth
- It allows the company to reinvent itself in response to customer needs and desires
- Continuous training corrects weaknesses, improves employee morale, and empowers employees to improve and grow
- Designing a continuous training program follows the same structure as that of initial training programs

- Just as with initial training programs, it is critical to create measurable goals and assess results

NOTES

Question: _____

_____

Question: _____

_____

Question: _____

_____

JERRY ISENHOUR

RIDE-ALONG TRAINING PROCESS

———— ◆ ◇ ◆ ————

A ride-along is also referred to as ride along coaching, and it is rightly called that. A blue-collar ride-along training is the reverse of what is called a ride-along in the white-collar world. For blue-collar professions, ride-along training is the process by which an employee goes into the field with a senior or more experienced employee, manager, or outside trainer with specialized skills, in order to learn about the process and operations of the company 'in real life'. In a white-collar ride-along, the manager or evaluator observes and, perhaps, offers assistance with a client. Most importantly, the presentation methods and habits of the white-collar professional are observed, and suggestions are made based on these observations. In a way, it is still training, but it focuses more on assessing and improving on the weaknesses of the rep and on commending the rep on the areas in which he/she excels, than on teaching the initial skills for the job.

In the case of the blue-collar technician, the main purpose of the ride-along is to teach the employee the process used to carry out a certain task, help them improve on the skills they already possess, and/or help them learn new skills. For a skilled worker, a ride-along could also be organized to observe how the staff goes about its duties, and critiques made to ensure your customers get the best experience.

A ride-along could be a single day in the field with the senior staff, or it could span weeks, months, even a year, depending on how hard it is to learn the new skill and the experience of the junior or new staff.

In many blue-collar jobs and roles, the worker can be both a technician and a sales person, and often they excel at one but not the other. The skills of sales and the skills of technical work are quite different, but as employers we frequently expect them to be phenomenal at both. This often is not the case and ride-along training can be the solution.

-Benefits of a ride-along training

For a company that wants to get the best performance from its employees, it has been established that employee training, including ride-along training, is one of the best ways to go about that. Here are some benefits of a ride-along training:

- ❖ **On-site learning experience:** The technician may have gone through a number of trainings: the in-house exercise, off-site training, even being trained by a contract trainer. There is just something about actually seeing the process of certain tasks being carried out that make the whole experience different. This is highly important for some learning styles; some people must not only hear it and see it; they also must do it. A new or junior staff person being able to ride along with a senior, more experienced staff member on a high-stakes operation will open their eyes to a whole new possibility of what can be achieved. For example, it is one thing to see a seventy-square meters base area twin electric furnace on paper and learning about all its operation, but it takes the learning process of the junior staff to a whole new level when he/she goes out in the field with a senior staff to carry out some maintenance on the furnace. Trust me, it is very enlightening.

- **Instant feedback:** During a ride-along training, the senior staff can get instant feedback from the junior employee concerning issues with the job. The ride-along in its own right serves as an on-the-job assessment mechanism, which would enable employee's mistakes to be quickly corrected, and their strengths easily recognized.

- **Builds an up-the-ladder relationship:** In most companies, the junior staff or new employee find it hard to build a relationship with their superiors. It is understandable since the superior may hold back from interacting with the junior employees, either due to pride or for self-preservation, fearing that they may jeopardize their position by educating someone who may wish to take their job. Therefore, the only time the senior staff have interactions with junior staff is when giving them orders or in some emergency meeting that involves all staff. The ride-along training method allows junior and senior employees to get to know each other on a professional, and to some extent personal, level since they will spend many days or even weeks together.

- **Better customer relationship:** A junior staff member, during a ride-along for a maintenance or repair call, would be able to learn first-hand how the company deals with customers. In every business, just as the skills of the staff are important, so too does the customer service philosophy determine the success of the company. So, a ride along with a senior staff member helps the junior staffer learn firsthand about the customer service culture of the company.

-How to conduct an effective ride-along

In this book, the word effective has been used quite a lot, and this is just to stress the importance of the training process of the company. It has to not only be good but also be effective for the company staff in every way.

A ride-along can be conducted in many ways; in fact, there are books that discuss it in detail. So, I will just highlight a few things necessary to make a ride-along effective.

- ❖ **Planning:** In life, nothing beats planning for things that need planning. Before the ride-along the senior staff person should know something about the junior staff person and what he/she needs to learn. Likewise, the junior staff person should be made aware of the upcoming ride-along training and be informed of what he/she can expect to gain from it. All the resources necessary to make the program a success should be provided.
- ❖ **Inform the client:** Sometimes the ride-along training will involve going to a client's place. If the client just expects one person, it could make them think their equipment is being used for practice. The client should be informed that the junior employee is on a training program and would be there mostly as an observer. This information should be relayed to the customer upon arrival at the site, possibly even before.

❖ **Time to discuss broader issues:** Even though individual growth is the primary focus of ride-along, Everett Hill of Catalytic Advisors recommends setting aside some time to discuss broader topics during the exercise. While the first part of the day might be focused solely on staff performance, it can be helpful to step back and discuss the overall picture towards the end of the day. The staff should always be aware of the larger goals of the organization and know how they contribute to them. Additionally, taking the time to talk about the future and the team gives the staff a break from individual criticism, which can be trying for certain personalities.

❖ **Set future goals:** Sales veteran and writer Wendy Connick suggests that managers should "decide on a measurable goal for the staff to achieve by the next ride" once a ride-along is over. She stresses the importance of setting a goal specific to the individual staff person's weakness, as opposed to the overall organizational weakness. For example, the employee might be great at installing new air conditioning units but weak with a specific task like repairing broken units, so setting a higher installation rate for them probably doesn't make sense. By addressing each staff person's individual setbacks, the overall organization will eventually reflect that change.

With all that has been talked about in this book, the training method used for an employee depends on a lot of factors and all these factors should be considered before choosing a training plan.

CHAPTER SUMMARY:

- Ride-along training allows new hires to learn by watching and doing in real-life situations
- Ride-alongs can be anywhere from one-day events to a program lasting for weeks, months, even a year
- Ride-along training creates a hands-on learning opportunity, allows for immediate feedback, builds relationships between new and senior staff, and exposes the new hire to the customer service philosophy of the company
- An effective ride-along requires planning; clients should be notified in advance
- The ride-along also allows time for discussion of broader issues and goal-setting

NOTES

Question: _____

_____

Question: _____

_____

Question: _____

JERRY ISENHOUR

THE VALIDATION PROCESS

———— ◆◇◆ ————

Validation is the process that assures that trainees have gained the skills and knowledge their training was intended to provide. Validation not only certifies the results of training but validates that the entire training program is designed correctly. After a training program, employees should have the skills to move on to the next step in their education or progress in their job. To properly validate the process, criteria must be set, and a system of tracking and measurement must be established.

Validation is a best practice that can provide both critical information about the return on investment (ROI) of a person and the system utilized in training, and as well as providing the data required to support it.

When it comes to validation, my experience shows that the biggest stumbling block is a lack of understanding of just what validation is and why it is so important. While the concept of validation has its complexities, it can be boiled down to a few simple concepts which are discussed below.

What is validation?

According to Dictionary.com, "validation" is defined as:

...to make valid; substantiate; confirm.

...to give legal force to; legalize.

...to give official sanction, confirmation, or approval to, as elected officials, election procedures, documents, etc.:

These definitions hold true when it comes to employment testing. Ask an Industrial/Organizational psychologist, and he or she will tell you that validation simply means the act of establishing two key things:

1. That anything used to make employment decisions is job-related, and
2. That the assessment measures what it is supposed to measure (i.e., that the test is "accurate").

There are a variety of ways to document the job-relatedness and accuracy of a test as a decision-making tool; however, a working understanding of validation should focus on two general types of validation: content validation and criterion-related validation.

At the very least, for a selection measure to be called content "valid" the test content must accurately reflect the skills needed for the job, so that the relationship of the test to the needs of the position can be documented.

This means that the job or jobs in question must be carefully evaluated and that the input of subject matter experts (supervisors and other assessment experts) be used to create a full understanding of the various things that are required for successful job performance.

Some of the content seems to be technical, but the purpose here is to make sure you get the general idea of how it works.

The process used to establish the job-relatedness of test content is known as "job analysis." Once information about job performance and related characteristics have been documented via job analysis, selection measures can be mapped out to match job requirements. For instance, if job analysis shows that the job requires fast and accurate bolt loosening and tightening, then the use of a bolt loosening test to hire applicants for that job is assumed to be content-valid based on its relation to job performance requirements.

Content validation is enough to satisfy EEOC requirements for claiming a test is valid (provided that proper procedures were followed). However, settling for only content validation is selling yourself way short. The real value proposition when it comes to validation lies in the evaluation of the ROI provided by a selection measure. This information can only be provided by criterion-related validation. So, what is criterion-related validation?

Criterion-related validation: Whenever possible, creating a statistical evaluation of the relationship between selection measures and valued business outcomes is desirable. This type of validation is known as "criterion-related validation," and it can provide concrete evidence of the accuracy of a test for predicting job performance. Criterion validation involves a statistical study that provides hard evidence of the relationship between scores on pre-employment assessments and valued business outcomes related to job performance. The statistical evidence resulting from this process provides a clear understanding of the ROI demonstrated by the testing process and thus helps document the value provided. Criterion-related validation also provides support for the legal defensibility of an assessment because it clarifies the assessment's accuracy as a decision-making tool.

In an ideal world, it is best to have both content and criterion validity evidence. Documenting content validity is a minimum requirement for any pre-employment selection measure; however, content validation alone can't provide any evidence for the ROI associated with a test or selection measure. Adding statistical validation bolsters the legal defensibility of an assessment *and* provides insight into ROI. Unfortunately, most companies do not perform criterion-related validation.

There are a few reasons for this:

- **Criterion study not possible:** A legitimate reason for not conducting validation studies is that there are simply not enough people in the job to allow for a reliable study to be conducted. The greatest shortcoming of statistical validation is the fact that its results are not credible unless the sample size is well over 100. Therefore, small companies and jobs with few experienced team members will lack the ability to gather criterion-related validation evidence.
- **Lack of resources:** Many companies feel that conducting criterion-related validation studies simply requires too many resources. They are not willing to spend the money needed or take the time to collect the data required to perform such studies.
- **Lack of understanding:** Many companies do not understand the concept of criterion-related validation and are not aware of the value it can provide so, therefore, they do not perform it.

- **Lack of guidance:** Test providers often sell tests as being "valid" because they have been validated for jobs similar to the one in question. While this may be true, it is not always an "out" that allows one to avoid doing criterion-related validation. Many test vendors do not provide advice or services related to criterion validation, leaving the user on their own to figure out this part of the equation.

What does all this mean to the professionals involved in the staff employment process?

- Educate yourself about validation and the options available to you.
- At a minimum, all measures used to select employees should be content-valid and job relatable. Failure to document content validity means the legality of your selection measures is compromised.
- Whenever possible, it pays to conduct criterion-related validation to add additional support for content validation efforts and to gain insight into the ROI of the selection measures.
- When reviewing tests provided by vendors, understand that a claim that a test has been "validated" can mean different things. Don't assume that, just because the test has been validated in another setting, it is automatically valid for your situation.
- Lack of proper validation for tests and selection measures can be costly! Citing lack of resources as a reason for not validating is like passing over dollars to pick up pennies.

❖ Both types of validation can add value. Content validation provides legal piece of mind, and criterion validation bolsters this and provides the ROI evidence needed to build a business case for using assessment.

As with anything else, it may take a bit of extra time and resources to do things right, but this extra effort will provide value and peace of mind. So, just keep experimenting with the process, and with practice and the use of the right tests you will get the results you are looking for.

CHAPTER SUMMARY:

- Validation certifies that a training has been successful and can provide valuable feedback about the return on investment (ROI) of both the trainee and the training program
- There are two general types of validation: content validation and criterion-related validation
- Employment testing must be content valid; it must test for skills or requirements of the job
- Criterion-related validation can provide concrete evidence that a particular test accurately predicts job performance
- Criterion-related validation requires a large sample size, significant resources, and a thorough understanding of the concepts involved, and so may not be usable in every situation
- Content validation protects you legally; criterion-related validation provides ROI evidence

NOTES

Question: _____

_____

Question: _____

_____

Question: _____

_____

JERRY ISENHOUR

CERTIFICATION AND LICENSING

———— ◆◇◆ ————

What are licenses and certifications?

Licenses and certifications show that a person has the specific knowledge or skill needed to do a job. Typically, you earn these credentials after you've completed your education. Sometimes, you become licensed or certified after you have gained practical experience, such as through an internship, residency, or time on the job.

Earning a license or certification involves meeting standards, which often includes passing an exam. Licenses and certifications are usually valid for a limited term and must be renewed periodically. An employer may require either credential. Usually, renewal of certifications or licenses require participation in continuing education classes and the collection of continuing education units (CEUs).

However, there are a few key differences in the way we use the terms certification and licensing. As shown below, one of the biggest distinctions between these two credentials is that licenses are legally required by the government to work in an occupation or to use specific intellectual property; certifications are not.

License

A license is an official permission or permit to do, use, or own something (as well as the document of that permission or permit).

A license may be granted by a party to another party as an element of an agreement between those parties. A shorthand definition of a license is "an authorization to use the licensed material."

Authorities may issue a license to allow an activity that would otherwise be forbidden. It may require paying a fee or proving a capability, but either way, a certain requirement must be met. There may also be a requirement to keep the authorities informed on a type of activity and they may set industry conditions and limitations.

A licensor may grant a license under intellectual property laws to authorize a use (such as copying software or using a patented invention) to a licensee, sparing the licensee from a claim of infringement brought by the licensor. A license under intellectual property commonly has several components beyond the grant itself, including **term**, **territory**, and **renewal** provisions, as well as other limitations deemed vital to the licensor.

Term: many licenses are valid for a specified length of time. This protects the licensor should the value of the license increase, or market conditions change. It also preserves enforceability by ensuring that no license extends beyond the term of the agreement.

Territory: a license may stipulate in what territory the rights pertain. For example, a license with a territory limited to "North America" (Mexico/United States/Canada) would not permit a licensee any protection from actions when used in Japan.

Renewal: a license with a specific term length will also usually provide the option of renewing the license. This may or may not include requirements for demonstration of competence or continuing education. For example, a driver's license typically does not require that you re-test every time you renew your license, but renewal of a real estate agent license often requires completion of continuing education coursework.

Another shorthand definition of a license is "a promise by the licensor not to sue the licensee." That means that, without a license, any use or exploitation of intellectual property by a third party would amount to copyright infringement. Such use would be improper and could, by using the legal system, be stopped if the intellectual property owner wanted to do so.

Intellectual property (IP) licensing plays a major role in business, academia, and broadcasting. Business practices such as franchising, technology transfer, publication, and character merchandising entirely depend on the licensing of intellectual property. Land licensing (proprietary licensing) and IP licensing form sub-branches of law born out of the interplay of general laws of contract and specific principles and statutory laws relating to these respective assets.

License properties include:

- ❖ Awarded by a governmental licensing agency or owner of the intellectual property being licensed.
- ❖ Gives legal authority to work in an occupation, or use a specific product or version of a product.
- ❖ Requires meeting predetermined criteria, such as having a degree or passing a state-administered exam.

Certification

A certification is a third-party attestation of an individual's level of knowledge or proficiency in a certain industry or profession. Certifications are granted by authorities in the field, such as professional societies, universities, or private certificate-granting agencies. Most certifications are time-limited; some expire after a specific period (e.g., the lifetime of a product that required certification for use), while others can be renewed indefinitely if certain requirements are met. Renewal usually requires ongoing education to remain up to date on advancements in the field, evidenced by earning the specified number of continuing education credits (CECs) or continuing education units (CEUs) from approved professional development courses.

Many certification programs are affiliated with professional associations, trade organizations, or private vendors interested in raising industry standards. Certificate programs are often created or endorsed by professional associations but are typically completely independent of membership organizations. Certifications are very common in fields such as aviation, construction, technology, environment, and other industrial sectors, as well as healthcare, business, real estate, and finance.

Types of certifications

There are three general types of certification. Listed in order of development level and portability, they are: corporate (internal), product-specific, and profession-wide.

Corporate, or "internal" certifications, are made by a corporation or low-stakes organization for internal purposes. For example, a corporation might require a one-day training course for all sales personnel, after which they receive a certificate. While this certificate has limited portability – to other corporations, for example – it is the simplest to develop.

Product-specific certifications are more involved and reference a product across all applications. This approach is very prevalent in the information technology (IT) industry, where personnel are certified on a version of software or hardware. This type of certification is portable across locations (for example, different corporations that use that software), but not across products. Another example could be the certifications issued for shipping personnel, which are under international standards for recognition of the certification body, the International Maritime Organization (IMO).

The most general type of certification is profession-wide. Certification is often offered by specialties. To apply professional standards, increase the level of practice, and protect the public, a professional organization might establish a certification. This is intended to be portable to all places a certified professional might work. Of course, this generalization increases the cost of such a program; the process of establishing a legally defensible assessment of an entire profession is very extensive. An example of this is a Certified Public Accountant (CPA), which would not be certified for just one corporation or one piece of accountancy software but for general work in the profession.

Certification properties include:

- ❖ Awarded by a professional organization or other nongovernmental bodies.
- ❖ May not be legally required to work in an occupation.

❖ Requires demonstrating competency to do a specific job, often through an examination process.

Sometimes, these credentialing terms are used interchangeably. For example, states may refer to the credentials teachers need as certifications. However, the Bureau of Labor Statistics would define them as licenses because they are issued by a state government and are legally required for many teaching jobs.

Licenses and certifications are more common in some occupations than others. Whether you need an occupational license or certification might depend on your state, company requirements, or the type of work your company does.

A higher-level academic education is often not required for many blue-collar jobs. However, certain fields may require specialized training, licensing, or certification as well as a high school diploma or General Educational Development (GED) certificate.

As the business owner, you will need to decide whether you will require certain voluntary validations, such as certifications, of your employees, either as a condition of employment or for advancement in your company. If, however, licensing is required by a governmental agency, that will require compliance. As such, you must research whether there are validations, such as licensing, required for work in your field. You will also want to research what voluntary validations are applicable in your field, and consider their value for your employees and your business. A company can use certifications held by their employees as marketing tools, to build market strength for the company and the company brand.

CHAPTER SUMMARY:

- Licenses typically grant permission to do, use, or own something

- Licenses are issued by governmental agencies or owners of intellectual property

- Certification typically documents an individual's level of knowledge or proficiency in a certain industry or profession

- Certifications are issued by authorities in the field, such as professional societies, colleges or universities, or private agencies

- It is critical that you are aware of what licenses or certifications are required to work in your field

- Employees holding voluntary certifications can be useful in marketing your business and building your company brand

JERRY ISENHOUR

NOTES

Question: _____

_____

Question: _____

_____

Question: _____

_____

JERRY ISENHOUR

SUMMARY

―――― ◆◇◆ ――――

The purpose of this book is to share with the reader some of the basic information required to implement a successful training process that can produce ROCK STAR QUALITY TECHNICIANS. As you have progressed through the book you have most likely found that this is not going to be an easy task, but with proper forethought, planning, and implementation, success can be achieved and your results can be phenomenal.

It will take a lot of work; there is no easy road. The successful implementer will devise a training system that works for their company, for new recruits and seasoned employees alike, and is presented in such a way that results can be measured. But this will require that you design the proper system.

There will also be the question of how do you instill this training in your staff; will it take the use of a big stick? Will it take a carrot for accomplishments? The answer will depend on the culture of your company and how you address the need for basic and continuing education from Day One. This will be contingent upon that all-important first day and the onboarding process. But it will also be contingent on your recruitment process and, most of all, on the way you share your company vision and culture with your new employee before they ever report for that all-important first day of work, as well as the surroundings the recruit is a part of and what the culture around him says.

It will also depend on the leadership skills you possess and how you lead others. I think it falls to the saying of President Dwight D. Eisenhower, "Leadership is the art of getting someone to do something because he wants to do it"!

This is where you, as the leader, must understand the goal and construct the strategy to fully attain that goal, both for you and those you are to train. Good luck in your endeavors.

ABOUT THE AUTHOR

Jerry Isenhour is a business coach, speaker, author, and educator. He has owned and operated businesses in the service, retail, and manufacturing segments since 1981. During his career as the CEO of multiple businesses, he also served in many industry associations and foundations as president, a member of boards, and as a committed volunteer. He started speaking, training, and writing in 1984 and has written numerous articles and presented classes and seminars around the United States on a variety of topics. In 2010, he formed Chimney & Venting Consultants and CVC Coaching, both serving business owners in the hearth, fireplace, chimney, and venting industry. He is also the owner of an online virtual training platform widely used in the chimney, venting and hearth industries. He serves as a resource to business owners across the United States.

In addition to this book, Jerry has published *Chaos to Reinvention* and *Standardizing Standard Operating Procedures*, both of which are available in printed and Kindle formats. He has also worked in collaboration with other authors on *The Daily Difference in Life Lessons; The Small Business Owner's Manual: Build Your Dream Business;* and *Blue-Collar Marketing: From Startup to Success*. Jerry is a certified member of the John Maxwell Team of Speakers, Coaches and Trainers. He also carries certification by Jeffrey Gitomer as a certified sales trainer and can offer aid and assistance to clients and their teams as a coach, a trainer, a consultant, and an analyst.

For more information about Jerry, check out his podcast, *The Chimney and Fireplace Success Network*, visit the websites www.cvcsuccessgroup.com, www.jerryisenhour.com, or find him on Facebook (CVC Coaching), Twitter (@JerryCvc), Instagram (@CVCJerry), YouTube (CVCCoaching), or LinkedIn (Jerry Isenhour). You can also reach him at jerry@cvcsuccessgroup.com